How to Encourage the Man in Your Life

H. Norman Wright

WORD PUBLISHING
Nashville·London·Vancouver·Melbourne

WORD PUBLISHING
Nashville, Tennessee

Library of Congress Cataloging-in-Publication Data

Wright, H. Norman.
How to encourage the man in your life / H. Norman Wright.
p.   cm.
ISBN 0-8499-1514-7
1. Marriage.   2. Marriage—Religious aspects—Christianity.
3. Wives—Conduct of life.   4. Encouragement.   I. Title.

HQ734.W94914   1998
306.85–dc21   97-45748
                                                                  CIP

Printed in the United States of America
7 8 9 BVG 9 8 7 6 5 4 3 2 1

The Woman Who Understands

Somewhere she waits to make you win, your soul in her
firm, white hands
Somewhere the gods have made for you, the Woman
Who Understands!

As the tide went out she found him
Lashed to a spar of Despair,
The wreck of his Ship around him—
The wreck of his Dreams in the air;
Found him and loved him and gathered
The soul of him close to her heart—
The soul that had sailed an uncharted sea,
The soul that had sought to win and be free—
The soul of which she was part!
And there in the dusk she cried to the man,
"Win your battle—you can, you can!"

Broken by Fate, unrelenting,
Scarred by the lashings of Chance;
Bitter his heart—unrepenting—
Hardened by circumstance;
Shadowed by Failure ever,
Cursing, he would have died,
But the touch of her hand, her strong warm hand,
And her love of his soul, took full command,
Just at the turn of the tide!
Standing beside him, filled with trust,
"Win!" she whispered, "You must, you must!"

Helping and loving and guiding,
Urging when that were best,
Holding her fears in hiding
Deep in her quiet breast;
This is the woman who kept him
True to his standards lost,
When, tossed in the storm and stress of strife,
He thought himself through with the game of life
And ready to pay the cost.
Watching and guarding, whispering still,
"Win you can—and you will, you will!"

This is the story of ages,
This is the Woman's way;
Wiser than seers or sages,
Lifting us day by day;
Facing all things with a courage
Nothing can daunt or dim,
Treading Life's path, wherever it leads—
Lined with flowers or choked with weeds,
But ever with him—with him!
Guidon—comrade—golden spur—
The men who win are helped by her!

Somewhere she waits, strong in belief, our soul in her
firm, white hands:
Thank well the gods when she comes to you—the
Woman Who Understands![1]

1. Jack Appleton Evarard, *The Quiet Courage and Other Songs of the Unafraid* (Cincinnati, Ohio: John G. Kidd & Son, Inc. Publishers, 1936), 15–16.

Contents

Introduction

Relationships—The very mention of the word elicits attention. Just look at all the books written today. They tell what to do, what not to do, how to do it, and how to get what you want without the other person knowing what you're doing. There seems to be a manual written for every type of man/woman interaction, and the majority seem to be written for women to know how to deal with men.

Well, this is not a manual, and it's not describing a series of subtle techniques designed to get your man to do your bidding.

This is a basic and simple book. It's not profound, although the message is thousands of years old. It's calling the reader to fulfill the biblical injunction to encourage—that's all—*encourage*. But encourage in such a way that your responses are uniquely adapted to that man in your life. By doing this your efforts connect with and meet his needs. Your belief in your man can be a source of continuing strength for his daily life.

The strength of this book comes from the men and women who shared their experiences. Their testimonies can open the doorway of understanding in this important means of reflecting our faith in Jesus Christ. There are positive results when we follow God's Word. I trust these will be an encouragement to you to reach out and be known as a woman who encourages.

Chapter

1

Who do you believe in? Who is the man in your life who would turn to you and say, "Thank you for believing in me"?

Chapter 1

~~~

Called to Encourage Your Man

Singer Kenny Rogers shared lyrics with a message, "She believes in me. Yes, she believes in me." These are words that can make all the difference in a man's life!

He gave credit where credit is due—to an encouraging woman. Every woman is given a power that can bring about change, growth, and the fulfillment of potential in another person, especially a significant man in her life.

Who do you believe in? Who is the man in your life who would turn to you and say, "Thank you for believing in me. It's your encouragement that makes my life different"? Listen to what these men say about how their wives encourage them.

~~~

"My wife encourages me by making herself available to help me with details I miss when I am under pressure because of my urgent projects. She makes sure that her schedule allows her to be a part of my life. I am able to trust her in everything. She is committed to building up our

1

marriage. She shows a genuine interest in what is important in my life, even if it isn't an interest of hers. What I desire from her is encouragement, and she's doing it!"

⁓

"She calls me several times a week at work to see how I am doing and to tell me that she has faith in me. That is very encouraging especially if I am struggling that day. She also calls to share her trials to give me a chance to encourage her. This in turn encourages me, because it makes me feel like she really cares about what I have to say. That makes me feel like she needs me."

⁓

"She understands my physical pain, supports me with her energy, and does what she can to take over some of the things I do to make life easier for me. She supports decisions I've made and helps in implementing and carrying out the course of action we've chosen. She's there to talk to and voice her opinion. We can talk about most things in an analytical way."

⁓

"My wife has been doing at least three things that I can think of to encourage me. Every time I do something that according to her was done very well, she makes positive remarks regarding these things. For instance, when I preach, she tells me how well she thinks I presented the message. When I've not done well, she makes me remember I can do it well. She helps me not to be discouraged by telling me she is sure that I will do better next time. To help celebrate my successes, she initiates a great night of love-making. That's a wonderful encouragement."

⌒⌒⌒⌒

"My wife encourages me by wanting to spend time with me going places I like to go (i.e. art shows, ball games, movies, etc.). She stays busy on her own doing something almost all the time (chores, time with kids, etc.). That's nice because I stay busy with other things or help with some of the same, and so the house runs smoothly without either of us being upset or critical of the other. She meets all my desires and needs in intimate ways. It's satisfying and something I look forward to.

"We talk every evening fifteen minutes to an hour, and she has both a listening ear and affirming responses, as well as an open and honest way about her. She is complimentary, faithful, loyal, dependable, and committed to making the marriage and family work. And our relationship is not a competition."

Not all the responses from men are positive. Some lament the lack of encouragement in their lives.

⌒⌒⌒⌒

"At the present time, my wife doesn't do much in the way of encouragement. I don't know if she doesn't want to or maybe I am not letting her. We have each other, we are both newly saved, we do talk about the Bible, and that is encouraging.

"I guess I would like to hear her say she loves me. She only says it if I do. So I say it a lot. When I have a bad day, I would like to relax. I just want to be supported in some of

3

my dreams. She is the best part of my life, I just want to learn how to encourage her better, too."

⁓

"My wife does not encourage me with words. I am verbal, and I do need that. I wish she would come and welcome me after I walk through the door at the end of the day. I wish she would say she is proud of me and that I do a good job. I wish she would truly grant me forgiveness when I confess a wrong to her and ask for it. A hug or an unexpected kiss on the cheek from her would encourage me greatly. I have been frustrated with her words and actions in the past, and we cannot seem to overcome that.

"I have never been unfaithful, but I might as well have had an affair. We have been counseled. The advice has been to give it time, let her see God changing me, love her as Christ loved the church. I am trying to do that. I have come to the conclusion that I can do anything for her. I hope the Lord changes her heart this year."

⁓

"There is no present encouragement. None! Her occasional praise for acceptably performed manual tasks is no encouragement whatsoever. I would be thrilled if she would simply acknowledge the legitimacy of my career and stop discouraging me from pursuing it. I would probably pass out from joy if she would go a step further and offer to seek ways in which I can pursue my calling with less impact on our family life."

The need for encouragement is there. And husbands have the desire to receive it.

There are many women who try to encourage the men in their lives, even think they are doing so. But it's difficult to be an encourager if we don't understand what encouragement really means.

To be an encourager you need to have an attitude of optimism. The *American Heritage Dictionary* has one of the better definitions of the word. It's a "tendency or disposition to expect the best possible outcome, or to dwell on the most hopeful aspect of a situation." When this is your attitude or perspective, you'll be able to encourage others. Encouragement is "to inspire; to continue on a chosen course; to impart courage or confidence."

Encouragement is sometimes thought of as praise and reinforcement, but it's also much more than that. Praise is limited. It's a verbal reward. It emphasizes competition, has to be earned, and is often given for being the best. Encouragement is freely given. It can involve noticing what others take for granted and affirming something others notice but may never think of mentioning. Bruce Larson shared this experience:

Early one morning I had to catch a plane from Newark, New Jersey, to Syracuse, New York, having returned late the previous night from leading one conference and on my way to another.

I was tired. I had not budgeted my time wisely, and I was totally unprepared for the intense schedule before me. After rising early and hastily eating breakfast, I drove to the airport in a mood that was anything but positive. By the time the plane took off I felt so sorry for myself.

Sitting on the plane with an open notebook in my lap, I prayed, "O God, help me. Let me get something down here that will be useful to your people in Syracuse."

Nothing came. I jotted down phrases at random, feeling

worse by the moment, and more and more guilty. Such a situation is a form of temporary insanity. It denies all that we know about God himself and his ability to redeem any situation.

About halfway through the brief flight, a stewardess came down the aisle passing out coffee. All the passengers were men, as women have too much sense to fly at seven o'clock in the morning. As the stewardess approached my seat, I heard her exclaim, "Hey! Someone is wearing English Leather aftershave lotion. I can't resist a man who wears English Leather. Who is it?"

Eagerly I waved my hand and announced, "It's me."

The stewardess immediately came over and sniffed my cheek, while I sat basking in this sudden attention and appreciating the covetous glances from passengers nearby.

All through the remainder of the flight the stewardess and I maintained a cheerful banter each time she passed my seat. She would make some comment, and I would respond gaily. Twenty-five minutes later when the plane prepared to land I realized that my temporary insanity had vanished. Despite the fact that I had failed in every way—in budgeting my time, in preparation, in attitude—everything had changed. I was freshly aware that I loved God, and that he loved me in spite of my failure.

What is more, I loved myself and the people around me and the people who were waiting for me in Syracuse. I was like the Gadarene demoniac after Jesus had touched him: clothed, in my right mind, and seated at the feet of Jesus. I looked down at the notebook in my lap and found a page full of ideas that could prove useful throughout the weekend.

God, I mused, *how did this happen?* It was then that I realized that someone had entered my life and turned a key. It was just a small key, turned by a very unlikely person. But that simple act of affirmation, that undeserved and unexpected attention, had got me back into the stream.[1]

Encouragement is recognizing the other person as having worth and dignity. It means paying attention to them when they are sharing with you. It's listening to them in a way that lets them know they're being listened to.

The road to a person's heart is through the ear. Men and women today have few people who really listen. When someone is talking most of us are often more concerned about what we are going to say when the other person stops talking. And this is a violation of Scripture. James tells all of us, men and women alike, to "be a ready listener." Proverbs 18:13 states, "He who answers a matter before he hears the facts, it is folly and shame to him."

Many of us have outgoing circuits, but the incoming circuits are clogged. One man was asked what his wife could do to encourage him. He said, "Listen. Listening without being judgmental or biased. Listening and accepting. Listening just to understand me. Listening instead of criticizing." But it's not just listening with your ears that's important but with your eyes as well. My profoundly retarded son, Matthew, only had a few words in his vocabulary. Joyce and I weren't sure if there were any meaning to those words. So we learned to listen to what he could not say by watching what he did, how he moved, and for flickering eye movements that indicated the onset of a seizure. Matthew taught me to listen in a new way that helped me better minister to the people I counsel.

Men and women have different listening styles, and it helps to understand what these are. Women tend to give more responses and feedback while they are listening. And these responses usually mean, "I'm with you" or "I understand" or "I'm connecting with you." On the other hand men not only say less, but their feedback usually means, "I agree with you." Have you run into this difference yet? Most women have. When you're listening to a man he may not need as much feedback from you as if you were listening to another woman. Listening quietly may lead to a response from him like, "Thanks for really listening to me. It helps me keep my mind on track when I'm not interrupted."

Encouragement validates that what the person is doing or saying makes sense. It's letting the other person know, "You matter to me." When you encourage, you respect the person as well. You rephrase negatives to positives by discovering the constructive elements in situations, such as identifying strengths and focusing on their efforts and contributions.[2]

This means you find something of value to recognize when everybody else has despaired! Encouragement is building up a person. It's focusing on any resource which can be turned into an asset or a strength.

It also means you expect the best out of a person. Consider what happened to this young man because his high school principal expected something more from him.

⌒

I remember vividly the day we had a school assembly. Three buddies and I went out behind the school auditorium. We all lit up. We knew we were safe: everyone else was in the assembly. And then, who should come around the corner but the principal. We were caught red-handed. My friends took off in three directions and left me just standing there. The principal collared me and dragged me down the hall in front of the auditorium just as the assembly was letting out. I thought I was going to die. Hundreds of kids saw me in this humiliating situation.

He took me into his office and chewed me out royally. It felt as if it lasted forever. Maybe it was only ten or fifteen minutes. I couldn't wait to get out of there. From that time on, I hated this guy. I waited for him to nail my buddies, but he never did. He knew who they were, but he did nothing. One day I saw him in the hall, and I asked why he hadn't gone after them. It wasn't fair that I was singled out.

Instead of giving me an answer there, he grabbed me by the collar, and dragged me back into his office. He sat me down, but the chewing out didn't even last a minute this time. I'll never forget what he said. "I wish your friends the best. I don't know what's going to happen to them, but you could be somebody. I expect more of you than this. You're coasting through life. When are you going to do something with what you've got?" He turned around and walked out. I felt like I had been slapped across the face. He was right; I was coasting. And there is only one direction you can coast—down.

I was a junior at the time. I started working a little bit in my classes and made a new group of friends. My senior year I had an A average. I had been getting C's and D's before. I decided I wanted to go on to college, but when I applied, I couldn't get in. My grades were too bad in a previous term. My principal wrote a letter of recommendation on my behalf, and in response the university agreed to admit me on a probationary status. I chose the field I did because of this man. He became like a mentor, like a second father to me.

Two years ago I gave the eulogy at his funeral. I'll never forget him. I will always be different because of him. He gave me something to live up to.[3]

Encouragement is not a deficit-oriented approach. To be an encourager, you need to go counter to our culture and not be "conformed to this world." We live in a mistake-oriented culture. We've become skilled as flaw finders. Would the man or men in

your life say you are more equipped to point out mistakes, weaknesses, or liabilities rather than strengths? The answer speaks
volumes!

Encouragement and acceptance often go hand in hand. This
older story dramatically illustrates what encouragement and
acceptance does for a man.

Peter Foster was a Royal Air Force pilot. These men
[pilots] were the cream of the crop of England—the
brightest, healthiest, most confident and dedicated, and
often the most handsome men in the country. When they
walked the streets in their decorated uniforms, the popu-
lation treated them as gods. All eyes turned their way. Girls
envied those who were fortunate enough to walk beside a
man in Air Force blue.

However, the scene in London was far from romantic,
for the Germans were attacking relentlessly. Fifty-seven
consecutive nights they bombed London. In waves of 250,
some 1,500 bombers would come each evening and pound
the city.

The RAF Hurricanes and Spitfires that pilots like
Foster flew looked like mosquitoes pestering the huge
German bombers. The Hurricane was agile and effective,
yet it had one fatal design flaw. The single propeller engine
was mounted in front, a scant foot or so from the cockpit,
and the fuel lines snaked alongside the cockpit toward the
engine. In a direct hit, the cockpit would erupt into an
inferno of flames. The pilot could eject, but in the one or
two seconds it took him to find the lever, heat would melt
off every feature of his face: his nose, his eyelids, his lips,
often his cheeks.

These RAF heroes many times would undergo a series

of 20 to 40 surgeries to refashion what once was their face. Plastic surgeons worked miracles, yet what remained of the face was essentially a scar.

Peter Foster became one of those "downed pilots." After numerous surgical procedures, what remained of his face was indescribable. The mirror he peered into daily couldn't hide the facts. As the day for his release from the hospital grew closer, so did Peter's anxiety about being accepted by his family and friends.

He knew that one group of airmen with similar injuries had returned home only to be rejected by their wives and girlfriends. Some of the men were divorced by wives who were unable to accept this new outer image of their husbands. Some men became recluses, refusing to leave their houses.

In contrast, there was another group who returned home to families who gave loving assurance of acceptance and continued worth. Many became executives and professionals, leaders in their communities.

Peter Foster was in that second group. His girlfriend assured him that nothing had changed except a few millimeters' thickness of skin. She loved him, not just his facial membrane, she assured him. The two were married just before Peter left the hospital.

"She became my mirror," Peter said of his wife. "She gave me a new image of myself. Even now, regardless of how I feel, when I look at her she gives me a warm, loving smile that tells me I am OK," he tells confidently.[4]

Time and time again we hear about the positive impact of an encouraging mother upon her son. I remember hearing an interview one day with Scott Hamilton, who has become a household name in professional ice skating. During the 1992 Winter Olympics Scott served as a commentator for the ice skating events. During his time on TV he shared about his special relationship with his mother, who died prior to his winning an Olympic gold medal. He said, "The first time I skated in the U.S. Nationals, I fell five times. My mother gave me a big hug and said, 'It's only your first National. It's no big deal.' My mother always let me be me. Three years later I won my first National. She never said, 'You can do better,' or 'Shape up.' She just encouraged me."

Another man said, "My mom was a very supportive person. She believed in what I could do even when I didn't. Oh, she gave her opinion and lots of advice but without being judgmental. And she cared about me as a person, not just what I did or could do. In time I felt I could do anything I set out to tackle. But the best thing she ever gave me was her unconditional love."

Encouragement means you show faith in the person and their potential. It's believing in them without the evidence that they are believable.

Perhaps you have a dream for that man in your life. You're able to see things that he can't see such as untapped potential. Have you ever heard of the four-eyed fish? It's an odd-looking creature to say the least. It's a fish native to the equatorial waters of the Western Atlantic region. Anableps is the technical name of this fish. (Just don't name one of your children Anableps!) It means, "Those that look upward" because of the unusual eye structure. This unique creature has two-tiered eyes. The upper and lower halves of each eyeball operate independently and have separate corneas and irises. So, if you were to confront one in its natural habitat, you would see him with his upper eyes protruding above the surface of the water. This helps him search for food as well as identify enemies in the air.

Now remember, this fish also has lower eyes. These stay focused in the water in the typical manner of most fish. On one hand the fish navigates in the water like other fish. But they have the advantage of seeing what other fish can't see because of the upper eyes. They see in both worlds. If you were like this, having four eyes, two for seeing what actually is and two for seeing what might be, you would be an unusual encourager![5]

John Maxwell, in his book *Be a People Person*, says we need to anticipate that others will do their best. "When working with people I always try to look at them not as they are but as what they can be. By anticipating that the vision will become real, it's easy for me to encourage them as they stretch. Raise your anticipation level, and you raise their achievement level."[6]

Perhaps the best way to describe encouragement is through the example of gardening. I've raised flowers and vegetables for years. Some years were good, others I'd rather forget! At times I've raised tomatoes. There's a right way to raise tomatoes and a wrong way. The right way is to make sure you have good soil with plenty of nutrients. You need water, cultivation, and fertilizers in the right amounts. You also need to stake the plant or use round wire cages for them to grow on. They need this support or their branches break. Sometimes you need to put up a protective cover and above all, watch out for insects, especially tomato worms.

After you've done all this you can take several weeks off to do nothing, right? No, you have to care for tomato plants consistently rather than sporadically, or you won't produce a crop.

Encouragement is like this. It takes work—constant, consistent work—for it to be effective.[7] When you're an encourager, you're like a prospector or a deep-sea diver looking for hidden treasure. Every person has pockets of underdeveloped resources within him. Your task is to search for these pockets, discover them, and then expand them. As you discover the strengths in your man you'll begin to focus on them. You'll look at them and care about what you discover. At first what you discover may be rough and imperfect. Talent scouts and scouts for professional sports teams do this all the time. They see undeveloped raw talent and ability, but they have the wisdom to see beyond that. They look into the future and see what can happen if all the potential were cultivated and developed. Do you? Is this what you do with your husband?

I found a poem which captures this idea in a unique way:

> God, through the years
> Of our married life
> You have been holding a crown
> About ten feet above my husband's head.
> He was simply too busy
> Loving and serving to notice.
> But I saw it.
> Not only did I see it—
> I watched him grow into it.[8]

Encouraging a person means you honor and respect him because you believe in him. And often your encouragement helps your husband or your fiancé live in such a way that he is worthy of being honored.

I entered sports late in life. I took up racquetball in my early forties. One of the reasons I kept at it was a young pastor who worked with me the first few months. I was a bit discouraged, especially when I noticed the proficiency of some of the younger men. But Tom was patient and excited whenever I did something right. He encouraged me; he believed in my ability; he saw me for what I could become, and that made so much difference. Now, almost twenty years later, I'm still playing. I have confidence, and some of those younger guys don't beat me anymore!

You are like the refiner's fire. What you notice and encourage can be refined in a positive way. Any movement that you see in a healthy, positive direction needs your attention and reinforcement.[9] You're saying, "Go for it. You can do it!"

One of the character qualities which lends itself to being an encourager is gentleness. This quality means that when we discover where another person is vulnerable or sensitive we're not hard, harsh, or forceful. When you discover a tender, sensitive place in your husband you protect it rather then step on it. As you consider ways of encouraging the man in your life, ask yourself:

- Am I gentle especially with those sensitive areas?

- Am I treating him the way I would want to be treated?

- Am I building hope in his life?

- Does he feel safe around me with those sensitive areas?

A Scottish poet, Sir Walter Scott, described the power of gentle words:

> Oh! Many a shaft, at random sent,
> Finds mark the anchor never meant.
> And many a word, at random spoken,
> May soothe or wound a heart that's broken.

A wife shared with me how she encouraged her husband to take some steps to move forward in his life. She said it would have been so easy to harp and criticize, which she knew would have a negative effect upon their relationship. She knew her husband had the ability to maintain himself in a healthy way, as well as complete his college degree if someone encouraged him. Here's how she did it.

⌒◡◠

"I worked hard to make good meals that were low in fat. I made only enough for two servings, so there weren't mounds of food sitting on the table begging to be eaten. I never bought junk food. My husband loves popcorn, and that became his snack food.

"Second, my husband is an excellent athlete who enjoys exercising when he has the time. He especially enjoys competitive sports. Although membership at a gym is expensive, I fully supported his doing this. Although he isn't fond of fast walking, I frequently asked if he would walk with me. He called these 'love walks.'

"Last winter, he decided he wanted a Nordic Track. For months we looked through the paper trying to find a used one, but finally I encouraged him to buy a new one. I'm glad we did it—he's gotten a lot of use out of it. Now his weight doesn't fluctuate twenty pounds every year, and he's in good physical condition.

"The next area of change was in my husband's education. My husband worked full-time during his college years, and it was impossible for him to finish his degree. Work always took priority over studies.

"After we had been married awhile, he was thinking about a job change but didn't feel confident that he was marketable without a college degree.

"We looked into a college program especially designed for working people. It was an intensive and expensive program that guaranteed a degree in a little over a year. At first my husband didn't want to do it. The money, the time, and the stress seemed overwhelming.

"I had taught some college courses and assured him I would help him every step of the way. I explained that we could finance his education if we kept to a strict budget and put off having children for another year. I promised to do most of the household chores and other responsibilities so he would have time to study.

"He entered the program. I typed papers, brainstormed

projects with him, helped him do library research, quizzed him at test time, and cheered him on through the entire year.

"He graduated summa cum laude! He has a degree and a good job. I don't believe he would have pursued this degree at this point in his life if we hadn't been married. My very presence in his life motivated him, because we were building a future together. I also think that my practical support eased the stress and struggle of that year. I'm thrilled to see his success."[10]

Perhaps you're like some women I've talked to, or I should say who have talked to me! They say, "Why do I need to be the one doing all the encouraging? I need it as much as he does, and I'm starving for some."

"This sounds just like what I've been hearing for years. Women have to give, give, and give. Sure we're nurturing but some men are spoiled. They're catered to all the time. If I do more of this, he'll just expect more!"

"This sounds one-sided to me. Many of us women go through life starving for some need fulfillment. Why don't you work with the men to get them to be more caring?"

These are good honest questions. I have two responses.

First, this is not a book directed to men. It's written to encourage women to encourage men. If it were written to men it would probably be even more direct than this one is! We, as men, have a great need to grow and develop as encouragers ourselves. In a relationship a man often functions as a thermostat. He affects the temperature of the relationship. Most of us men were raised emotionally handicapped and relationally deficient, and I'm saying that as a collective response for men. We have much to learn! And men can and do learn. But there are other books and helps for men. This one is basically for women.

Secondly, as Christians we don't really have any choice about whether we encourage others or not. It's not our decision to make. Scripture states that others will know that we are Christians by the love we show for one another. And one of the ways we reflect this love is by being an encourager. Look at what God's Word tells us to do.

In Acts 18:27, the word *encourage* means "to urge forward or persuade." In 1 Thessalonians 5:11 it means "to stimulate another person to the ordinary duties of life."

Consider the words found in 1 Thessalonians 5:14, "And we earnestly beseech you, brethren, admonish (warn and seriously advise) those who are out of line—the loafers, the disorderly and the unruly; encourage the timid and fainthearted, help and give your support to the weak souls [and] be very patient with everybody—always keeping your temper."

Scripture uses a variety of words to describe both our involvement with others as well as the actual relationship. Urge *(parakaleo)* means "to beseech or exhort." It is intended to create an environment of urgency to listen and respond to a directive. It is a mildly active verb. Paul used it in Romans 12:1 and in 1 Corinthians 1:4.

The word translated encourage *(paramutheomai)* means "to console, comfort, and cheer up." This process includes elements of understanding, redirecting of thoughts, and a general shifting of focus from the negative to the positive. In the context of the verse, it refers to the timid ("fainthearted," KJV) individual who is discouraged and ready to give up. It's a matter of loaning your faith and hope to the person until his own develops.

Help *(anechomai)* primarily contains the idea of "taking interest in, being devoted to, rendering assistance, or holding up spiritually and emotionally. It is not so much an active involvement as a passive approach. It suggests the idea of coming alongside a person and supporting him. In the context of 1 Thessalonians 5:14, it seems to refer to those who are incapable of helping themselves.

First Thessalonians 5:11 states, "Therefore encourage one

another and build each other up, just as in fact you are doing" (NIV).

Hebrews 3:13 says we're to "encourage one another every day." In the setting of this verse, encouragement is associated with protecting the believer from callousness.

Hebrews 10:25 says, "Let us encourage one another." This time the word means to keep someone on their feet who, if left to himself, would collapse. Your encouragement serves like the concrete pilings of a structural support.

One of my favorite verses is Proverbs 12:25. "Anxiety in a man's heart weighs it down, but an encouraging word makes it glad."

The Word of God is very clear about what we're to do. To be a consistent encourager you will need to reflect the character qualities of 1 Corinthians 13. Here they are amplified in a unique way.

- Patient (tolerant of frailties, imperfections, and short-comings of the man in your life)

- Kind (tender, thoughtful toward your man)

- Not jealous (of genuine friendships with others or of the special gifts and talents of your husband)

- Not boastful (about personal appearance or achievements in an attempt to compete with your man)

- Not arrogant (not disdainful of your mate's looks or achievements; don't belittle your husband)

- Not rude (not inconsiderate of your man's needs or feelings)

- Not insistent on your own way (willing to compromise, to consider your man's needs and interests)

- Not irritable (don't snap at your husband; approachable)

- Not resentful (don't hold grudges; forgiving)

- Don't rejoice in wrong (don't delight in your man's misfortunes; don't keep score or tally perceived wrongs)

- Rejoice in right (truthful; don't try to conceal things from your man)

- Bear all things (support your man in times of struggle)

- Believe all things (don't challenge words of your man)

- Hope all things (don't wallow in pessimism about your relationship; keep a positive attitude)

- Endure all things (don't give in to pressures of life; willing to stand by your man when he's having personal struggles)[11]

One man described why he felt encouraged. He said, "I was reading the Scriptures one day and found this passage. It summed it all up better than I could say it."

> A good woman is hard to find,
> and worth far more than diamonds
> Her husband trusts her without reserve,
> and never has reason to regret it
> Never spiteful, she treats him generously
> all her life long. (Proverbs 31:10–12, MSG)

Hopefully you're already encouraging the man in your life. The results may amaze you!

Chapter

2

What happens when a man is not encouraged?
A discouraged man ends up feeling hopeless,
helpless, and handcuffed to his situation in life.

Chapter 2

◦⁓◦

The Discouraged Man—
He's Not a Pretty Sight

He sits in the chair in front of the TV. You can't tell from the expression on his face whether he's actually watching it. Is he awake? In a daze? Or even breathing? He's oblivious to the world around him. His body is in the chair, but that's about all. The rest of him seems to be elsewhere. He has things to do and many responsibilities. He used to be alert, creative, functional, productive, and enjoyable to be around. Not now. Something happened, and it can happen to all men. For some, it's occasional or periodic. For others it's a daily routine that can come and go. The condition? Discouragement. You know what I'm talking about. You've been there. We all have.

What happens when a man is not encouraged? A discouraged man ends up feeling hopeless, helpless, and handcuffed to his situation in life. He feels stuck, immobilized, and impotent. He can end up seeing himself as a loser, unable to solve problems or find solutions to the challenges of life. Confidence in his own abilities is absent. Life is unfair, and the scales are constantly tipped against him. The pessimistic expectations he develops can set him up for failure.

A discouraged person makes assumptions. Unfortunately these are not made in his favor. He assumes he's inadequate, a failure, and has very little worth. He believes others see him this way as well.

Some men live in a constant condition of discouragement. They want to be affirmed, recognized, treated with respect, have their accomplishments appreciated, and be validated. They want to feel they've made a contribution to life. But when they don't, watch out. It's not a pretty sight! Discouraged men tend to start looking for some ways to get all of the above, but their methods can be counterproductive. They can actually bring about more failure while they're pursuing the desired affirmation.

A discouraged child or an adult who isn't being recognized and given sufficient attention often becomes overbearing, loud, and even obnoxious in order to get attention. It doesn't work. It just invites more rejection. So they intensify their efforts. The results? More rejection.

It may be that the signs of discouragement are all around your husband, and you can't see them. You've labeled them something else. Sure, there could be other reasons for these signs. There could even be some serious disorders, but for now consider these as SOD—"signs of discouragement." When you see these signs in your man, they have just the opposite effect on you. The last response you want to give is encouragement! You're turned off.

Some men need an audience—constantly. They have to be the center of attention. It doesn't matter whether it's positive or negative. They want all eyes focused on them. If there's no audience, there's no show. They need the attention of others to affirm themselves. Some of their actions could be bizarre, inappropriate, or even shocking. That doesn't matter as long as they have your attention. Any reaction is better than none. I've seen some men who as children were the class clowns. It didn't matter that others laughed at them or didn't think much of them. You may have been drawn to such a man because he made you laugh. But everyone who laughs reinforces the attention-getting behavior and keeps the man learning to get attention in unhealthy ways.

What do *you* tend to encourage by *your* attention? The healthy positive responses or the inappropriate? Some men (and you may be thinking *all men!*) have an excessive need for power and control. They seem to feel secure or reassured only when they're in control. Being in control gives them the sense of encouragement that they don't receive from others. After all, who feels like encouraging someone who overrides or dominates you? The greater the need for power and control, the greater the hidden feelings of inadequacy and inferiority.

When this man is in the driver's seat he feels important, even adequate, for a little while. He may have been pampered as a child. Weren't we all to some degree? But into his adulthood he carried with him the belief that everyone else will do unto him as his parents did. So he lives with constant frustration because the world doesn't operate that way. He intensifies his efforts, leaving little room for behavior that would bring the encouragement and positive responses he wants.

Sometimes men use dishonesty to get attention. It's repugnant to most of us, so we focus on the behavior rather than the cause. We all hate to be lied to. It breaks our trust, and we feel violated. And yet a discouraged man may lie for several reasons. His encouragement container is running on empty so he resorts to dishonesty. It's an easy way to gain attention. His prevailing rationalization is that the truth isn't that important, and he won't get much response if he's truthful. Listen to Jim's experience.

"Even after I married I felt a bit left out. Everyone else seemed to have a life that was more significant or important.

When others talked people responded, but when I shared anything it seemed boring. So I began to embellish just about everything. It worked. I learned how to point out accomplishments that really meant very little. But I got praise and encouragement. One day I got caught in these lies . . . by my wife. It was hard telling her how insignificant I felt. She was shocked. She thought since I was so quiet and easygoing I was secure. Little did she know. But how could she? I never told her."

Most of us don't equate perfectionism with a feeling of discouragement. But perfectionism is the great cover-up. It's a way to camouflage a wide variety of self-perceived weaknesses. Perfectionists live with the fear of failure so they take steps to try to assure that failure will never happen. They live in a self-imposed prison and can become their own worst enemies.

The expectations they have for themselves and for you are unobtainable. They've got to have a safe, secure, and predictable environment. Often they either don't receive much encouragement because of being difficult to live with, or else they may not believe the encouragement they do receive. They'll point out their own mistakes that you're not even aware of. These are people who need affirmation for who they are rather than for their endless striving. They need encouragement for any relaxed normal interaction. Since blame probably helped create this condition, they certainly don't need to be blamed for the way they are.

Have you interacted with a man who was close-minded? You know, the kind who wouldn't consider any other possibility and had an opinion for everything? The more close-minded a man is, the more discouraged he may be. It's his way of trying to create a safe world. He doesn't want to change because that would be an admission that what he did or thought may have been wrong. He wants a predictable, safe world. He doesn't want to be wrong and this is his way of avoiding greater discouragement.

Some discouraged people go into a protective cocoon. They retreat from both the challenges and the interactions of life. They create a safe environment and only allow safe people to join them. They're just the opposite of the attention seekers. If anyone wants to compete, they avoid the situation. If they're encouraged or pressured by their wives to try to get ahead at work, they ignore the request. They're very compliant, agreeing with anyone and everyone. It's hard to know what they believe and what they stand for. It's true that some men are somewhat this way because of their personality bent, but often competition to a discouraged man is just another experience where he will lose and someone else will be affirmed. He thinks, *Why risk it? It's not worth it.*

One of the frustrations many women face is having to deal with a man who won't take responsibility. The lack of initiative, avoidance, and passive-aggressive responses can be a pattern for numerous reasons. But think about it for a moment. If you were discouraged, would you really want to take on responsibility? It's just another possibility to have something go wrong, and you end up bearing the criticism.

When a discouraged person does make a mistake, he's very adept at placing the blame on others. Sometimes this person lives by a rule book. It's safer when you don't stray from the guidelines. Usually he avoids making decisions or judgments. Too much could go wrong. In some ways he appears rigid, inept, and irresponsible because he fails to take ownership. It's very easy to fall into the trap of letting such people become dependent upon you.

It's not surprising that a discouraged man has a lack of confidence. We need to remember that discouraged people have little courage. They've lost what they had in the first place. So why would we expect them to reach out and try? When you're discouraged your perception of life changes. You're not motivated to be a risktaker. Your belief and faith in yourself is low, and your need for others to believe in you is higher than usual. When you're discouraged you don't expect success. You don't expect the best—you expect failure.

A forty-year-old man summed it up when he said, "I've been discouraged for some time. I'm discouraged about my job, my kids, what I've done with my life. . . . I know I've acted in some dumb ways but I just don't know any other way to act when I'm this discouraged. There's probably something else I could do that's better, but I can't think of what it is, and nobody else is showing me. And that discourages me even more."

Remember, whether the man in your life is a husband, fiancé, father, or son, when he's discouraged his main concern is not how to break out of the discouragement pattern, but how to look good and secure, and not appear weak and inadequate.[1]

Whether a man finds fault with others or whether he's on the receiving end, it's discouraging. Faultfinding is a common form of criticism and a favorite pastime of the perfectionist.

Do you know why faultfinding is so destructive in any relationship?

Faultfinding deeply wounds the man. Constant verbal and nonverbal criticism says, "I don't accept you for who you are at this time in your life. You don't measure up, and I can't accept you until you do." In more than twenty-five years of counseling I have heard multitudes of people in my office cry out in pain, "My spouse's criticism ripped me apart. I was made to feel like dirt. I never felt accepted, and I'm still looking for someone who will tell me I'm all right."

Faultfinding also wounds you. The wounded person becomes afraid or angry and retaliates through overt or covert withdrawal, resentment, or aggression.

Faultfinding really doesn't change the other person. Though he may appear to change his behavior in response to criticism, his heart rarely changes. He may simply learn to cover his rebellious attitude with external compliance.

Faultfinding is contagious. A faultfinding person teaches intolerance to the other person by example. Thus the person learns to be critical and unaccepting of himself and others.

Faultfinding accentuates negative traits and behaviors. When you pay undue attention to a person's mistakes or irresponsible behaviors, you tend to reinforce them instead of eliminate them.[2]

Criticism is usually destructive, but it's interesting to hear critics say they're just trying to remold their partner or child into better persons by offering some constructive criticism. But too often criticism does not construct, it demolishes. It doesn't nourish a relationship, it poisons. And often the presentation is like this description: "There is one who speaks rashly like the thrusts of a sword" (Proverbs 12:18, NASB).

Criticism that is destructive accuses, tries to make the man feel guilty, intimidates, and is often an outgrowth of personal resentment.

Criticism comes in many shapes and sizes. You've heard of "zingers," those lethal, verbal guided missiles. A zinger comes at you with a sharp point and a dull barb that catches the flesh as it goes in. The power of these sharp, caustic statements is seen when you realize that one zinger can undo twenty acts of kindness. That's right, twenty. And men don't handle these very well.

A zinger has the power to negate many positive acts. Once a zinger has landed, the effect is similar to a radioactive cloud that settles on an area of what used to be prime farmland. The land is so contaminated by the radioactivity that, even though seeds are scattered and plants are planted, they fail to take root. Subsequently they die out or are washed away by the elements. It takes decades for the contamination to dissipate. The kind acts of loving words following the placement of a zinger find a similar hostile soil. It may take hours before there is a receptivity or positive response to your positive overtures.[3]

Another form of criticism is invalidation, which is often the cause of destroying relationships. When invalidation exists, it destroys the effect of validation. Sometimes people get along and maintain their relationships without sufficient validation, but they cannot handle continual invalidation. This is yet another example of one negative comment canceling twenty acts of kindness.[4]

Invalidation is like a slow, fatal disease that, once established in a relationship, spreads and destroys the positive feelings. As one man said, "The so-called friend I married became my enemy with unexpected attacks. I felt demeaned, put-down, and my self-esteem slowly crumbled. I guess that's why our fights escalated so much. I had to fight to survive." To keep love alive, keep the criticism out of it. God's Word has something to say about this.

Instead of just being critical when a problem occurs, perhaps you could respond like the pilot in this story as described in the magazine *Flight Operations*:

Bob Hoover, a famous test pilot and frequent performer at air shows, was returning to his home in Los Angeles from an air show in San Diego. At three hundred feet in the air, both engines suddenly stopped. By deft maneuvering he managed to land the plane, but it was badly damaged. Thankfully no one was hurt.

Hoover's first act after the emergency landing was to inspect the airplane's fuel. Just as he suspected, the World War II propeller plane had been fueled with jet fuel rather than gasoline.

Upon returning to the airport, he asked to see the mechanic who had serviced his plane. The young man was sick with the agony of his mistake. Tears streamed down his face as Hoover approached. He had almost caused the loss of a very expensive plane and could have caused the loss of three lives as well.

You can imagine Hoover's anger. One could anticipate the tongue-lashing that this proud and precise pilot would unleash for the carelessness. But Hoover didn't scold the mechanic; he didn't even criticize him. Instead, he put his big arm around the man's shoulder and said, "To show you I'm sure that you'll never do this again, I want you to service my F51 tomorrow."[5]

Can you think of a time when you've responded to the man in your life in a similar way?

You can be a discourager by being either passive or active. Passive discouragement comes through the lack of encouraging your man. It's like existing in a vacuum. Direct criticism is active discouragement. You may not be a critical person, but everyone has complaints at some time or another; that's normal.

Complaints can be voiced in a way that won't stir up defensiveness and can actually be encouraging. For example, instead of focusing on what bothers you, talk more about what you would appreciate the other person doing. He's much more likely to hear you and consider your request if you are positive. Talking about what you don't like just reinforces the possibility of the undesirable behavior continuing with an even greater intensity. The principle of pointing toward what you would appreciate also conveys your belief that he is capable of doing what you have requested. Doing this consistently, along with giving praise and gratitude when he complies will encourage him and could bring about a change.

The power of praise cannot be underestimated. I've seen this in children as well as adults. I've also seen this principle work in raising our golden retriever, Sheffield (not that I'm comparing people to dogs). Sheffield was trained in the basics by the time he was four months old, and now he brings in the paper, takes items back and forth to Joyce and me, "answers" the phone and brings it to me, and picks up items off the floor and puts them in the trash. All it took was ignoring the times when he didn't do it right and giving praise and hugs when he came through. He learned that we believed in his ability to accomplish what he had been trained to do.

I don't think people are much different in this respect.

31

Affirming and encouraging responses can literally change a person's life, because we all want someone to believe in our capabilities. An unusual example of this is found in the Babemba tribe in southern Africa. When one of the tribal members has acted irresponsibly, he or she is taken to the center of the village. Everyone in the village stops work and gathers in a large circle around the person. In turn, each person, regardless of age, speaks to the person and recounts the good things he has done in his lifetime. All the positive incidents in the person's life, plus his good attributes, strengths, and kindnesses, are recalled with accuracy and detail. Not one word about his problem behavior is even mentioned.

This ceremony, which sometimes lasts several days, isn't complete until every positive expression has been given by those assembled. The person is literally flooded by positives. When the people are finished, the erring person is welcomed back into the tribe. Can you imagine how all this makes him feel about himself? Can you imagine his desire to continue to reflect those positive qualities? Has there been a time when you've done this with your husband or father or son?

Criticism is the initial negative response that opens the door for the other destructive responses to follow. Criticism is different from complaining because it attacks the other person's personality and character, usually with blame. Most criticisms are overgeneralized ("You always . . .") and personally accusing (the word *you* is central). A great deal of criticism comes in the form of blame, with the word *should* being included.

Criticism can be hidden under the camouflage of joking and humor. And when confronted about it, the person will avoid responsibility by saying, "Hey, I was just joking." It reminds me of the passage in Proverbs that says, "Like a madman who casts firebrands, arrows, and death, so is the man who deceives his neighbor and then says, 'Was I not joking?'" (Proverbs 26:18–19).

Some men are very adept at discouraging themselves. In fact, some are masters at it. They have found ingenious ways to keep themselves crippled and stuck.

But often a man is discouraged because of the responses from others—often those closest to him. Most of the ways of discouraging others are quite subtle. I don't know of too many who make it a point to discourage others purposely. But it happens. *What every man needs is an abundance of encouraging responses and an absence of discouraging ones.*

How might a woman discourage the man in her life? You can dominate him (or try to). Remember that domination stifles growth. It deadens initiative. It takes away the opportunity for others to take on responsibility, grow, and mature. We can dominate others by always being there and giving our "strength" to help them.

Continuous statements like, "Let me do that" or "This is the way that goes" or "Honey, don't try. I'll get someone who's an expert on that" could contain the subtle message, "You'll mess it up; let me do it." Redoing tasks that a man has done has several possible outcomes. It could convey to him it's never good enough for you. He could end up thinking, *Why put forth a lot of effort, she'll just redo it anyway if I mess it up. After a while, she'll quit asking.* It's possible for any of us to end up letting another person get away with halfhearted attempts keyed by our responses.

Encouragement means that we believe in the other person's potential to learn to do something adequately (perhaps not perfectly or your way). It also means having the patience to work with them as they learn while showing we believe in them. If you're a parent you know how long it can take for your child to learn and refine a task. Whether you're dealing with a child or an adult you want to work yourself out of a job by letting the other person do things that you're already proficient in doing.

You need to have trust and confidence in the other person's abilities. It could be at this point you're saying, "Yes, but . . . you don't know the man I'm dealing with." You're right, I don't, but we don't want to limit him by a belief that he can never be different than he is now!

Sometimes a woman can discourage a man by her insensitivity. He's excited about something, and you show no interest. He wants you to do something with him, and you're too preoccupied with your tasks. He asks you how his new shirt and tie look, and the look on your face speaks volumes. If your husband suggests that you have devotions together you respond with, "Finally, after ten years you come around. Well, who suggested that to you?"

Another way we discourage people is by our silence. I've heard women say, "When I affirm or compliment him all I get back is a grunt, so I've stopped." "If I encourage him it will just go to his head. His ego is overinflated as it is." "I would think the satisfaction that he gets from what he does at work from others would be enough." "I don't know why my husband is always asking me, 'How did I do?' or 'What do you think?' I always like what he does and think it's great. You'd think he'd remember what I said the time before!"

Silence can be loud. It has its own sounds, its own volume. It often says, "I don't care," "You're not important," "I can't be bothered." Silence can hurt more than words.

Your man won't know what you believe and feel about him unless you tell him.

Remember, one of the biggest discouragements for a man is the feeling that he has failed in something, or is responsible for a problem his wife has. A man tends to assume that when a woman talks to him about her problems, the reason she does is because he's the culprit. So he becomes defensive or rattles off numerous solutions. He needs to hear that he isn't the cause, and all he needs to do is listen to you. When you want his opinion, a hug, a kiss, or just his attention, let him know. One man said, "I feel so comfortable and relaxed in my marriage. We both do a lot for the other, but one of the biggest helps my wife gives me is disarming me in advance. She lets me know what she wants or needs when she talks to me, and I've learned through this not to assume or be defensive. If she needs to confront me when I've blown it, I can handle it so much better now because of the relationship we worked out over the years. I really feel supported by her."

Let's consider the process of discouragement in marriage. Many men struggle with need fulfillment. Dr. Willard Harley (partially out of his own experience) identified five basic needs men expect their wives to fulfill and five needs women expect their husbands to fulfill. Often the failure to meet each other's needs is based on ignorance rather than refusal. We may live in a country that has a high literacy level, but many of us are basically illiterate about relationships and the fine art of understanding our mates. There really is no reason for married couples not to be fulfilled today.

What basic areas of need and fulfillment did Dr. Harley suggest? First, men cannot do without sexual fulfillment. This should come as no surprise to anyone.

The second need may surprise you. Men want their wives to spend recreational time with them. Recreational compatibility is very important, and it must be carefully cultivated because tastes vary. Men tend to enjoy activities that involve more risk and adventure than women do. Men often fear that if their wives join them, their activities will be limited. Wives usually pressure husbands to spend their spare time with the family. This can build resentment. What works best for most couples is actually having his and her recreational activities, but putting an emphasis on shared activities. My wife and I enjoy fishing together, but many times she encourages me to go fishing with my friends on the more intensive rugged trips.[6]

A third need according to Dr. Harley is for the wife to be attractive. This does not mean she has to be beautiful, but she should strive to maintain the level of attractiveness she had when they married. Of course, this should apply to men as well. I have seen as many men as women let themselves go after they marry.

A fourth need is for peace and quiet. Moms need time to recoup, recharge, and rebound—but so do dads. Couples need to discuss when this should occur so both are satisfied. Too often this becomes a source of tension and argument in a marriage and degenerates into a pursue/withdraw conflict.

The fifth area of need is admiration. One man shared his thoughts well:

Many writers and therapists have pointed out the need that men have for admiration and respect. As one husband said, "Because of men's high need to accomplish, they are in need of more positive encouragement than most women seem to understand. I have observed some wives withholding praise from their husbands because they either thought their husbands did not need more praise or that others were doing a sufficient job already. Many wives fail to notice the desperate search by their husbands for honest acknowledgment of their efforts. One of the best gifts from God is a spouse who acknowledges, encourages, and supports her partner as a natural habit. One of the blessings from my wife that has a great impact on me is when she speaks well of me to others. This is particularly true when she doesn't think I'm listening, or when I find out indirectly what she has said to someone. We all want to be well thought of, and when our wives become our "public relations managers" we experience honor from them, which is truly humbling.[7]

Men thrive on honest admiration from women. We desperately need recognition and encouragement. Men and women need to specifically identify their own unique needs and make a point of sharing them with their mates.

If you're married, consider the top ten intimacy needs in a marriage. When these needs are met, usually satisfaction is realized by both husband and wife.

Top Ten Intimacy Needs in a Marriage

1. *Attention*

    Attention means to think about the other person, to focus on him by listening with your eyes and your ears in addition to showing interest, concern, and support. It's a bit like entering into the other person's world.

    What Paul said about the body of Christ—the Church—applies also to marriage: "That there should be no division in the body, but that its parts should have equal concern for each other" (1 Corinthians 12:25).

    If you share a request for attention, say what you need, what the other person's attention will do for you, and how it will improve the overall relationship. This way of speaking can be a form of encouragement since it shows you believe he can do it. Above all, don't attack, indict, or blame.

2. *Acceptance*

    The best description I have heard of the quality of acceptance in love is more than twenty years old. "Acceptance," this source said, is "an unconditional commitment to an imperfect person." The men in your life are imperfect. You obviously know that. True acceptance means deliberate, positive, and ready reception. As Paul said, "*Accept* one another, then, just as Christ accepted you, in order to bring praise to God" (Romans 15:7, NIV, emphasis mine). In what way can you show the man in your life acceptance?

3. *Appreciation and Praise*
Each of us needs appreciation and praise. Appreciation is gratefulness that is verbalized. In most marriages, however, the norm is to take your spouse for granted.

Make a list of every single helpful or positive thing your husband does or has done. Then enumerate the times you have shared your appreciation for each one. Too often we are aware of what our partner has not done rather than what he or she has done. We have to look for the positives and reinforce them with praise if we want them to continue. Marriages that are satisfying are those in which there are five times as many positive exchanges as there are negative. Remember what the apostle Paul said in 1 Corinthians 11:2: "I praise you for remembering me in everything and for holding to the teachings, just as I passed them on to you" (NIV).

4. *Encouragement*
You see, it's a basic need for everyone. That's one reason for a book devoted to this subject.

5. *Support*
The need for support in intimacy is described in the Bible as "bearing one another's burdens." This means discovering exactly how your husband would like to be supported—not doing what you think is best. It can also mean giving a hug rather than a solution, putting dinner

on hold so he can unwind for a half-hour, or reflecting on and clarifying his responses rather than saying you are too tired to talk.

A counselee shared with me how his wife blessed him one day through her caring support and friendship. Phil, a man in his thirties, had been under intense pressure and stress for several weeks. His new job was a disaster because delays and unreasonable demands from his supervisor were wearing him down. Added to this, Phil and his wife had moved two thousand miles away from home to take the job, and both sets of parents continued to express their displeasure about the move.

One particular day, everything was going wrong at work. In addition, Phil's parents called him at work to dump on him for abandoning them. As he was walking out at quitting time, his supervisor informed him that he would have to work the following Saturday.

When Phil arrived home he was totally dejected. His nonverbal signals screamed discouragement. He told me later, "I felt shattered, discouraged, and unable to please anyone." He immediately headed for his chair and slumped into it in silence.

When Phil's wife entered the room, she could read his nonverbal signals and knew it had not been a good day. Phil explained what happened:

> Eileen just came over to me and stood behind me, gently stroking my hair and massaging my stooped shoulders. All she said was, "Would you like to talk about it or not?" Her sensitivity, her touch, her willingness to give me the freedom to talk or not talk encouraged me so much. I didn't feel all alone anymore. I knew I had someone who would stand by me even in my discouragement. I felt blessed. In fact, I know I am blessed in having such a wife.

Many of the responses in our surveys were from men requesting this kind of support. "Carry each other's burdens, and in this way you will fulfill the law of Christ" (Galatians 6:2).

6. *Affection*

Affection is a basic ingredient of marriage. It can mean anything from a sexual interchange to a nonsexual touch. Touch is communication.

Affectionate touching generates the sensations of warmth, security, and emotional satisfaction craved by every human being. Patting, stroking, and caressing carry the nonverbal message of endearment and tenderness that we all need beginning at birth. That physical need does not diminish when we grow into adulthood.

No amount of cultural restriction or stereotyping can eliminate the need for physical contact, although Americans tend to be less "touchy" in relationships than people from other cultures. Travel to Europe, Africa, or Asia and you might be surprised to find how adults hug, hold hands, and lean against each other.

Helen Colton cites in her book *The Gift of Touch* the observations of a social scientist who contrasted the touching habits of Americans with those of the French. Within an hour's time, French friends touched each other about one hundred times, while the Americans touched no more than three or four times. Touching is an expression of affection. How frequently does your husband need to be touched?

7. *Approval*

Every husband and wife looks for approval from a spouse. Romans 14:18 reminds us, "Because anyone who serves Christ in this way is pleasing to God and approved by men" (NIV).

Approval is giving positive affirmation, or thinking and speaking well of someone. It can be expressed in a word or a look.

God models approval for us in His Word. What he said to Moses, He says to us: "I am pleased with you" (Exodus 33:17, NIV). God takes pleasure in you! He even rejoices over you in song (see Zephaniah 3:17).

Married couples are to approve of each other. You have a choice: You can look for something to approve of, or you can look for something for which to disapprove. "Love," Paul wrote, "is ever ready to believe the best of every person" (1 Corinthians 13:7).

8. *Security*

   Security involves trust. It means you can depend on the one you trust. You can rely upon that person's word. You can count on that person to back you and to praise you not only in your presence, but also when you are not there. You know that person is doing what is best for you. Psalm 15:4 speaks of people who inspire security and dependability by saying, "They keep their promises, no matter what the cost" (NLT).

9. *Comfort or Empathy*

   Having someone who understands us, identifies with us, and can therefore comfort us is an important need. It is also an admonition from Scripture: "Therefore encourage each other with these words" (1 Thessalonians 4:18, NIV); "Rejoice with those who rejoice; mourn with those who mourn" (Romans 12:15, NIV).

Comfort consoles in a way that touches the heart of the other person. Comfort can be different for each of us, therefore we need to understand what brings comfort to our mate. Comfort can be expressed in words, silence, actions, sex, holding each other, etc.

When you empathize with someone, you enter into the experience with that person. You gently come alongside the other person, matching his or her pace. You see through the other person's eyes. When you fail to empathize, your partner feels disappointed and rejected.

When a man is hurting, his wife needs to be especially sensitive to his needs. It is important for a wife to determine whether her husband needs privacy or attention. It is equally important for her husband to tell his wife what he needs. Offering him unsolicited advice often makes matters worse. It sends the message that he can't or won't figure out the problem for himself. Because being competent is important to him, he tends to be touchy about this. He hears it as a criticism. Instead, his wife should ask him if he would like to hear her suggestions.

If you are trying to be comforting or empathetic, remember that men and women tend to handle their problems and struggles differently. Exceptions do exist, but in general the following differences will be prevalent.

- Men usually need to put the problem on the back burner, think about it, and find a solution.

- Men do not readily have answers to their wives' questions or even their own problems when asked.

- When men are upset or stressed, talking may not be helpful.

- Men tend not to want to say anything they might regret later. Silence (for a while) may be necessary.

10. *Respect*

Although both men and women need respect, men seem to need it more than women. When you respect people, you value them. You have a high regard for them, and you honor them. "Love each other with brotherly affection and take delight in honoring each other" (Romans 12:10, TLB).

Belittling, correcting, and giving too much unsolicited assistance diminishes respect. Paul wrote:

> However, let each man of you (without exception) love his wife as [being in a sense] his very own self; and let the wife see that she respects and reverences her husband—that she notices him, regards him, honors him, prefers him, venerates and esteems him: and that she defers to him, praises him, and loves and admires him exceedingly. (Ephesians 5:33)[8]

It is important for a healthy marriage to continue to grow—forever. Love does not have to die. It wants to live. We kill it through neglect.

One of the best ways to keep from falling into the trap of discouraging others is to live out God's Word in our lives. Following these two passages will certainly point you in the right direction.

> Let all bitterness and indignation and wrath (passion, rage, bad temper) and resentment (anger, animosity) and quarreling (brawling, clamor, contention) and slander (evil speaking, abusive or blasphemous language) be banished from you, with all malice (spite, ill will, or baseness of any kind). And become useful and helpful and kind to one another, tenderhearted (compassionate, understanding,

loving-hearted), forgiving one another [readily and freely], as God in Christ forgave you. (Ephesians 4:31–32)

———◦———

Clothe yourselves therefore, as (God's own picked representatives,) His own chosen ones, [who are] purified and holy and well-beloved [by God Himself, by putting on behavior marked by] tenderhearted pity and mercy, kind feeling, a lowly opinion of yourselves, gentle ways, [and] patience—which is tireless, long-suffering and has the power to endure whatever comes, with good temper. Be gentle and forbearing with one another and, if one has a difference (a grievance or complaint) against another, readily pardoning each other; even as the Lord has freely forgiven you, so must you also [forgive]. (Colossians 3:12–13)

Chapter
3

When understanding occurs relationships change and blend, and both the man and woman can be fulfilled.

Chapter 3

To Encourage Him, You Have to Understand Him

Differences! They've been praised and cursed, glorified and condemned, identified as adding richness to relationships as well as being blamed for the demise of many marriages. But they exist. They always have and always will. Some differences are slight and some are extreme. Differences are not the problem in a relationship. Identifying, understanding, and accepting them is not what creates friction and misunderstanding. So, if you want to encourage a man you need to understand him.

The Book of Proverbs is filled with practical wisdom about life. One of the main themes is the value of developing understanding.

"Incline your heart to understanding"(2:2, NASB).

"Understanding will watch over you"(2:11, NASB).

"Call understanding your intimate friend" (7:4, NASB).

"Wisdom rests in the heart of one who has understanding"(14:33, NASB).

"A man [or woman] of understanding walks straight" (15:21, NASB).

"Understanding is a fountain of life to him [or her] who has it" (16:22, NASB).

~~~

Understanding is not an end in itself. But it's an important vehicle to give you wisdom and direction. Understanding helps you feel for another person, to identify with his struggles and difficulties. And, something that is especially critical with a man, it helps you know what to say and what not to say as well as when to say and when not to say something. Often the development of acceptance is tied into your level of understanding.[1]

Understanding seems to go hand in hand with another word, *empathy*. When you understand and are empathetic you put yourself into the thinking, feeling, and acting of another person and in a sense structure your world as they do. It's as though we are in the driver's seat of the other person's vehicle, experiencing life as they do. It is viewing the situation through their eyes. Two biblical examples of this are Galatians 6:2 and Romans 12:15, which admonish us to bear one another's burdens, to rejoice with those who rejoice, and weep with those who weep.

It is not only difficult to separate understanding from empathy, but it's even more problematic to separate it from love.

I like the way J. B. Phillips clarifies the meaning of the love we're to have for one another:

~~~

> This love of which I speak is slow to lose patience—it looks for a way of being constructive. It is not possessive, it is neither anxious to impress nor does it cherish inflated ideas of its own importance.
>
> Love has good manners and does not pursue selfish advantage. It is not touchy. It does not keep account of evil

or gloat over the wickedness of other people. On the contrary, it is glad with all good men when truth prevails.
Love knows no limit to its endurance, no end to its trust, no fading of its hope; it can outlast anything. It is, in fact, the one thing that still stands when all else has fallen.
(1 Corinthians 13:4–8)

For more than thirty years I have seen major misunderstandings in male/female relationships because of the lack of understanding and acceptance of differences. These differences exist because of gender, personality, and learning styles. The longer I study and counsel, the more I'm convinced that these three have an integral blended relationship with each other. It's difficult to say that a man is a certain way just because he is male. He is that way because of gender, personality, and learning style. When understanding occurs relationships change and blend, and both the man and woman can be fulfilled.

In order to encourage a man you need to understand his uniqueness so your efforts at encouraging him can be designed to fit him.

I've heard many women say they understand men, but few actually do. They have beliefs about them, but many of those beliefs are based on stereotypes as well as cultural myths.

Listen to the words of one man:

> We believe women don't fully understand that men are different from women. They appear to realize they are different from us, but they don't understand how different we are from them—and that it is good that we are different. The difference is not a negative. Let's keep in mind that God created us differently for a purpose. And it is good. We don't want to be like women.

Take gender differences, for example. Often they're puzzling, baffling, and one of the reasons for conflict. Instead of feeling like an ally with that man in your life, you feel like an adversary.

Several years ago I had an experience that dramatically demonstrated gender differences in both thinking and communication style. Joyce and I were visiting historical Williamsburg, Virginia. It's a fascinating and charming setting that preserves and portrays colonial history.

One day we decided to take the tour of the old governor's mansion. Our tour guide was male. As we entered the large entry hall, he began to give a factual description of the purpose of the room as well as the way it was furnished. He described in detail the various antique guns on the wall and pointed to the unique display of flintlock rifles arranged in a circle on the rounded ceiling. When he said there were sixty-four of them, some originals and others replicas, I immediately began counting them (a typical male response). Our guide was very knowledgeable, and he gave an excellent detailed description as we went from room to room. He seemed to be very structured and focused.

We had to leave before the tour was complete to meet some friends for lunch. Since we both enjoyed the presentation so much, we decided to return the next day and take the tour again. What a difference! Our guide was a woman. As we entered the same room as the previous day she said, "Now, you'll notice a few guns on the wall and ceiling, but notice the covering on these chairs and the tapestry on the walls. They are . . ."And with that she launched into a detailed description of items that had either been ignored or just given a passing mention the day before. And on it went throughout the tour.

It didn't take much to figure out what was going on. It was a classic example of gender differences. Our first tour guide was speaking more to men and the second one more to women. Actually, we ended up with the best tour imaginable because we heard both perspectives. What a benefit it would be for the guides to incorporate both approaches into their presentation.

This example of differences can be seen time after time. What you are going to read now I've written about elsewhere in much more detail (*Understanding the Man in Your Life* and *How to Bring Out the Best in Your Spouse* with Dr. Gary Oliver; see chapters 4–9). You may have read about men from other writers' perspectives, but it's important to summarize some of the unique features of a man. This will help you know how to adapt your encouraging responses.

Make a list of the characteristics of the man in your life. What is he like? Does he behave differently around other people? Look at your list again. This is a road map providing you with the directions you need to encourage him.

Let's hit the main issue right away: feelings and emotions. Recently I came across a fascinating book by Michael Gurian, *The Wonder of Boys.* I wish every parent could grasp the information in this book. One section was entitled, "How Boys Experience Their Feelings and Emotions." (Keep in mind the reason for these male/female differences goes back to the presence of testosterone in men as well as the difference in the brain structure.)

Boys have eight internal processing methods for experiencing feelings and emotions. And you may see this in the men in your life as well. They have an *active-release approach.* They process and express their feelings through some sort of action like a game or activity or even yelling. Have you ever seen this occur?

Then there's the *suppression-delayed reaction method.* A male is wired differently. Whereas a woman may verbally process a problem aloud immediately, men are basically wired for more of a delayed reaction. A man's brain is a problem-solving brain, so emotional reactions are delayed until the problem is solved. He could be irritable at this time but doesn't talk about the problem. Perhaps you've experienced this in your relationship with your husband or father or son.

Men also engage in the *displacement-objectification method.* Perhaps a boy or a man is angry. You want him to talk about it but he won't. He might first talk about how someone else or feels in a particular dilemma. Once he does that, he may then talk about how he feels.

Boys tend to make objects even of their feelings since that's safer. One boy saw a dog chained up. He said, "Boy, what a life. He's tied down and stuck there. Can't go where he wants to and feels everybody is pulling his chain. Sometimes that's the way I feel when . . ."

Once again, he needs more time to deal with the feelings. That's how you can encourage him. He may need you to help him connect his feelings to the outside world. A wife realized that her husband had a difficult day at work because he was unusually quiet. Although his responses were unusually short, she discovered he had an overload of problems at work. So she said, "It sounds like you had an experience today like the red sports car I read about at the wild animal park."

He said, "What are you talking about?"

"Well, it's that drive-through park where the animals roam around. A guy drove through in a real small red sports car and one of the elephants who had worked in a circus saw it. He came over and sat down on it like he had been taught to do in the circus."

Her husband replied, "You couldn't have put it any more aptly. I felt today just like that car, except my elephant jumped up and down a bit!"

Yet another method of dealing with feelings is the *physical expression method* which boys use much more than girls. Exercise and games provide some of the outlets for their inner feelings. Again you can see how men use action rather than words. You've probably heard the expression, "Going in the cave" approach. Several writers, including John Gray, the author of *Men Are from Mars, Women Are from Venus,* address this issue. On the average, boys don't process their feelings as quickly as girls. Sometimes it takes them several hours to do so. (You may be thinking, *It's more like days!)* And they can become overwhelmed by a woman's feelings. They prefer isolation so they can sort out their feelings. They need to know it's OK to go into the cave, and it's okay to come out of the cave as well. Do you know a cave dweller? If so, do you try to drag him out of the cave or encourage him to enter it and stay there awhile?

There's another method men use called *talking about feelings.* It's often easier for a boy or a man to talk about the feelings after an event rather than during it. You need to remember that it is just physically more difficult for men to express feelings because of their brain structure. This isn't an excuse. It's the way God created males and females. It was His idea. You can encourage a man to talk about feelings, but what may come natural for you could feel awkward for him.

The *problem-solving method* is a process that often releases a boy's emotional energy. This is why you can expect the man in your life to move this direction as quickly as possible. You may talk it out, but he wants to solve. Seeing a problem creates feelings. When the problem is solved, he will feel much better.

The *crying method* feels unsafe to boys or men. Culture has helped to keep the tears pent up. Men do cry, but many of them can only cry on the inside. Only a few feel comfortable enough to express tears. The feeling of loss of control when this happens is an unpleasant exposure and vulnerability for most men.[2]

Men are very skilled at covering up their real feelings. They have numerous ways of hiding their emotions. For example when a man is sad, fearful, hurt, or feeling guilty he may use anger to avoid the pain of those feelings. When he's angry he feels more like he's in control. And since most people don't feel like getting close to someone who is angry, he is able to maintain a safe distance.

Then when a man is truly angry, to get away from the pain of those feelings, he may use discouragement or indifference as his Novocaine.

When a man is insecure, uncertain, feeling ashamed, or

actually afraid, anger is useful to avoid facing those feelings. He may turn his anger into aggression to overcompensate for other feelings he can't safely express.

One of the most frequent translations of one feeling for another is the exchange of anger for frustration. One other factor to remember about men and anger:

> A man's low self-image is usually the result of threats of an interpersonal nature, such as insults or undue criticism. Studies show that men with a high sense of self-worth are much less affected by criticism.
>
> Insults and criticism are especially provocative of anger if the man already suffers from low self-esteem, instability relating to poor social adjustment, depression, anxiety, and low life satisfaction. These men usually did not receive the affirmation they craved from their fathers during childhood, and they get angry when they are not affirmed and appreciated as adults. No matter how hard he tries, the man with low self-worth never quite measures up to the idealized vision of what he thinks others expect him to be. He may appear to be quite confident and secure, but in reality he is insecure and highly sensitive to the criticism of others, positive or negative.
>
> A man's anger in response to his low self-worth serves a number of functions. It prompts him to express his displeasure at the affront he has suffered. It helps him defend himself against all his negative feelings. It encourages him to restore his wounded self-esteem and public self-image by going on the offensive. Yet in the process of trying to save his own skin, he may bring pain to others, especially those closest to him."[3]

One of the best responses you can give a man about what he is experiencing or feeling is validation. Do you understand what this word means? It's the process or act of confirming or supporting the meaningfulness and relevance of what your man is feeling. It's listening, understanding his perspective. It's walking with him emotionally without trying to change the direction he's going.[4]

One of the mistakes some women make is to edit their own feelings because they believe their man can't handle them. They try to protect their husband, father, or son from their pain when they're upset. If you hold back your feelings because your man has difficulty handling them, you're not helping the relationship, you're creating an emotional distance. It will leave you starving for emotional connection—from anyone! This is one of the reasons why some women stray from their husbands.

When you edit or block your feelings, you begin to lose your own identity. You may end up being unsure of whether you are the person who experienced that emotion, or whether you're another person who is tying not to feel it. It's like asking, "Who am I?""Who's the real me? The one who feels or the one who doesn't feel?"

The result is some women don't encourage their men with positive affirmations because of the confusion they have over their feelings.[5]

There's another range of differences and that has to do with personality. Let's look for a moment at Frank, who may be like a number of men (or women) you know.

Frank likes his life precise, structured, and regulated. When he asks you a question he wants to hear a precise definite response, not something that is vague or general. He tends to correct others when they tell a story because he is a stickler for details. He likes to see results in whatever he does. His attitude toward many situations in life is, if it isn't broke, why try to fix it? Leave well enough alone.

He is bottom line in how he says things as well as being very linear in how he thinks. He breaks the problem down into pieces and goes through steps 1, 2, 3, and 4 to find a solution. Frank just loves structure. He likes to put things in order by regulating, organizing, enumerating, and fitting things into rules and patterns.

Because of his gender-based brain uniqueness and personality, he can be very focused. Perhaps this concept is new to you.

A male's brain is organized with a high level of lateralization. Men tend to shift farther left or right than women do. And there are some who make equal usage of both sides, since neither side is dominant.

Is there a generic right-brain/left-brain difference between men and women? Yes. This is part of the answer to why men and women are the way they are. A man's brain is more highly specialized. If I am a typical man, I will use the left side of my brain for verbal problems and the right side for spatial. This latter area tends to help men excel over women in a sport like baseball because a man can better perceive the relationship between ball and bat. If I am putting together a new barbecue grill which came in pieces, I use my right brain to visualize the end result. Thus I shift from one side to the other. I am seeing how it fits together in my mind. If my wife, Joyce, comes to discuss who we are having over for dinner, I respond out of my left verbal side.

Personally, I feel we men do not use all the abilities of the right side as much as we could. The emotional, intuitive side in men is often stunted, partly due to a lack of socialization training and encouragement and partly because of our tendency to use one side of the brain or the other at a time but not as much in conjunction.

A woman is different in the way she uses her brain. And it gives her an advantage over men! A woman's brain is not specialized. It operates holistically. A man shifts back and forth between the sides of his brain. He can give more focused attention to what he is doing. But a woman uses both sides of her brain simultaneously to work on a problem. The two parts work in cooperation. Why? Because some of the left-brain abilities are duplicated in her right brain and some of the right brain in the left. Women have larger connectors between the two sides, even as infants, and can integrate information more skillfully.[6] In addition, women have 40 percent more connectors between the left and the right sides of the brain.[7]

The way in which men use their brains is an exclusive mode. (Some women refer to it as tunnel vision!) It can exclude everything except what he is focusing on. It shuts out other possibilities. And men exert an abundance of energy to stay in this position. Most men like to know exactly where they are and what they are doing at a given point in time. It's a way to stay in control.

Life seems to revolve around them. They like the sameness of their environment. It gives them security and is less of an energy drain when things stay the same. If a man walks into his living room and the furniture has been rearranged, his wife may be delighted but he is bothered because he has to reorient himself. If he wasn't notified of the change in advance, he feels even more out of control. And he works to get back in control.

So if your husband is at home and his attention is locked on the TV, the newspaper, or fixing the car, he's in his exclusive mind-set. If you talk to him, he feels an interference or intrusion. And for him it's an energy leak. He hopes it will leave! For most men, when they're working on a project or a task at home, it's not a fellowship time for them. When he does exert energy to shift from whatever he was doing to concentrate on you, he's upset because of the energy expenditure. He has to change his focus and shift it elsewhere because he can't handle both at once. You may feel he's inconsiderate for not listening, and he feels you're inconsiderate because of the intrusion. Actually, neither is. You just don't understand the gender difference. If you did, you could each learn to respond differently.

Listen to what four different men said about this issue:

"Many of us would like to communicate with our wives as intimately as they communicate with their friends. But we find it difficult. Who will help us learn? We receive few offers—only complaints."

⌒

"Women say we are single-minded. We are. Single-mindedness helps us reach our goals. We have difficulty listening when we are concentrating on something else. We are accused of being purposely inattentive and made to feel guilty and even attacked for this. Why?"

⌒

"We want women to understand that we need more time to process what is said to us than women do. When we feel pressured to be different, we may use anger as our protection—to get others to back off."

⌒

"She expects me to have these reactions right at my fingertips and be able to call them up on the spot. Well, I can't do that. I don't operate the way she does. I need a little more time to think things through. I don't want to say something I'm going to regret later on. Somehow she has the idea that wanting time to think is not being open and honest with her. That is ridiculous! I'm not trying to hide anything, I'm just trying to be sure in my own mind before I talk to her about it."[8]

Frank doesn't like to use his imagination very much or consider options. He likes the here and now. He's great at home when it comes to putting things together. He reads the instructions from front to back and then follows them step by step. Shopping for him is a task! He doesn't go to enjoy the process.

It's something to be conquered. Usually he'll call the store to see if they have the needed item. He prefers to go in, money in hand, pick it up, pay for it, and walk out never seeing any other items.

His philosophy of life is to work now and play later. Organized? That's his middle name. He wakes up in the morning, and you wonder if he didn't plan his day while he slept. He knows what he will do that day. He has a schedule, follows it, but comes unglued if things don't go the way he planned them. If a surprise or change comes into his life, watch out! He has a place for everything. And guess what? He's not satisfied until everything is in its place!

He likes order and special systems for keeping things in the garage, his fishing kit, hangers in the closet, shirts color-coded in order in the drawer and his pens nearby arranged in order on the desk. His playtime is organized and so are his times of spontaneity! He might plan a week in advance to be spontaneous on a Saturday afternoon from one to four. Not only is he decisive but bothered by those who can't seem to make up their minds.

So . . . does this sound like anyone you know? Or maybe the man you know is just the opposite. But if this man sounds familiar to you, how would you go about encouraging him? What would you say or do?

Let's consider how to communicate with Frank. One of the ways to encourage a man is not to frustrate him when you talk with him. You've probably figured it out already.

When you share with him keep it brief, simple, focused, bottom line, result- and task-oriented, linear, orderly, not too many options, relatively free from change or surprises. Get the picture? You are probably thinking his life is sterile, boring! "That's not my personality!" you say. "That's not the way I live my life!" That may be true. But a man who is like this and knows his wife is the opposite will be encouraged when he sees her making the effort to adapt and learn to speak his language. (Hang in here, ladies. If this book were for men, I would be asking the man to adapt to your style when he speaks with you!) He is more likely to hear you and appreciate you. Even words of encouragement need to fit this adaptive pattern.

Listen to Ed, married several years to Sue, as he shares his desire to be encouraged.

⌒

"I'd like to tell you about my outgoing wife. She's a real talker. She talks and talks. She even talks to herself. I'm just the opposite. I don't talk much at all. At first I was attracted to her talking. Then I was repulsed by it. My ears get exhausted.

"I couldn't understand why Sue had to think out loud so much. It's like she wanted the whole world to know about her wild ideas. And it's not just because she's a woman. I've seen men who are the same way. But it seemed like she would start talking before she engaged her brain. At times I felt like my space was invaded by her giving a running commentary on everything or saying the same things over and over or wanting an immediate response from me on a question I'd never had a chance to think about. That wore me out. I began to feel she didn't want to hear what I had to say.

"There were even times when I'd go to the garage to putter around (and find some peace and quiet), and Sue would come out there, bring up a subject, ask my opinion, arrive at her own conclusion before I could think about it, thank me, and walk out. I'd just stand there shaking my head and wonder, *Why even ask me?* I felt invaded and unimportant.

"When we went to an activity, it was like she knew everyone there and wanted to stay forever. It seemed like she would never run down or get enough socializing. I've seen men like that too. I always wondered how they did it.

It drains me but seems to give her a shot of adrenaline! I'd like to leave early, but she doesn't understand I'm exhausted by people.

"Something else used to bother me—Sue is better about this now—she would interrupt me when we talked. It takes me longer to get things out and reach a conclusion. So, if I talked or thought too slowly, I either got interrupted or she finished my statement for me. We had a good discussion (argument) over that one. But she's much better now, and I don't avoid discussions with her. Sometimes I remind her that our speed of thinking and speaking is different and that helps. That's when I'm encouraged about the relationship.

"When we have a conflict I think (or used to think) there was just too much talking about the problem. Sue had the belief that if we just talked it through a bit more, everything could get resolved. Resolved! A few more words would be the last straw. We eventually learned to put some time limits on each segment of the conversation so I could have time to think. Then I was ready to continue. I also worked on sharing my first reaction without having to do so much thinking and editing. When she's patient it helps me work on myself.

"Now and then I've said to her, 'I want to resolve this, but since I'm getting worn down, why don't you write out what you're thinking or put your thoughts on the computer? Then I can read them over and be able to reason out my response.' That's worked well for us. That way Sue doesn't get as loud either, since I really tend to withdraw when that happens. I used to tell her, 'You're not going to get me to respond by shouting at me. It won't work.' Now I say, 'I want to hear you. I would appreciate it if you would say it softly and give me a chance to respond.'

"Sometimes I would ask her, 'Why are you bringing that up again? We've already talked about it.' Sue would say, 'No, we haven't.' And then we'd argue over whether we had or not. This went on for years until one day I heard her say, 'Could it be that you rehearse conversations in your mind and then think that we've already talked about it?' Bingo! That's exactly what I was doing, and when she said it, I realized she was right. Fortunately, we've learned to laugh about it. Sometimes I catch myself and say, 'Yeah, I did talk to you about it . . . in my head.'

"What has really helped me (and us) is to realize that there's nothing wrong with Sue the way she is. That's just her. It's the way she's wired. I guess it's the way God created her. We're just different and are learning to adjust.

"I've learned to appreciate the fact that she's encouraged me to be more social and involved with other people, and I've discovered I can be. It's become apparent that Sue needs more interaction and time with people than I do. Now I'm glad to provide it. It's all right for her to go places and gab, and I can stay home or get together with one of my male friends.

"It's really helped me to understand that Sue needs to talk out loud to figure things out. And it doesn't mean that she's going to do what she's thinking out loud. She's just thinking. I've learned not to assume.

"We're not perfect, but we are much more accepting. We've learned to be creative in the ways we approach each other. Being married to her has structured me. It's helped me relate to others. And I see her accepting who I am more and more."

Now let's hear what Sue has to say about her relationship with Frank.

"I'm an outgoing, talkative person who for some strange reason was drawn to a quiet, reserved, thoughtful man. I loved him and wanted to be his helpmate. I knew we were different when we were dating, but I never realized just how much until we were married. When it really hit me was the evening I figured out that Frank seemed to be avoiding me. Even when I was talking to him it seemed like he couldn't wait until I quit talking. And his responses became shorter and shorter. It was as though he thought if he said less I wouldn't have so much to respond to. I guess it was true, because eventually I'd get fed up and socialize on the phone. I actually felt rejected and hurt because I wasn't getting enough conversation out of Frank. I couldn't figure out why he was like that. At first I thought, *That's just the way men are.* But other men I had dated weren't always like that. In fact, I've known women who act like Frank. So I figured it's just the way he's wired.

"I do enjoy getting together with others. I am energized by them. But it doesn't take long (at least it seems to me) for Frank to get worn out at a party and want to leave early. I've even seen him just sit off to one side by himself or go into another room for a while just to be alone. I used to think, *What is wrong with that man?* Then, I began to discover that Frank needs some quiet time and space to get his energy back. That's draining for me, but it perks him up. So I figured if this is who he is, let's work out some ways I can encourage him. Frank's friendly and communicates well, but he doesn't go out of his way to connect with people. I've had many friends, but he's satisfied with just two. There's the difference—just two! That wouldn't be enough for me. I need more people to talk with.

"One of our biggest conflicts was in the area of communication. I like to get things resolved. That means talking through every part of an issue. But when we talked, or when I talked, the more he seemed to retreat. So I figured I'd just keep after him and he was bound to open up. No such luck! He'd retreat, clam up, or say, 'I don't know.' I admit, I want answers right now. I used to say, 'Frank, tell me right now. You don't need time. For Pete's sake, tell me!' And then nothing. Silence. It's like I just short-circuited his thinking ability. And later on I discovered I had! I wasn't letting him be who he really was!

"I've discovered Frank is more of what they call an inner person. Through some reading, I discovered he's the kind of person who likes to think things through in the quiet privacy of his mind without pressure—and then he's got a lot to say! I didn't know this at first. Now when I need his feedback or a discussion, I just go to him and say, 'Frank, here's something I'd like you to think about. Put it on the back burner where it can simmer for a while, and when it's done, let's discuss it.' He appreciates it, and we talk more. After I did this for a while, he told me, 'Thanks for recognizing and respecting my need to think things through in the privacy of my mind.' That felt good, because I like compliments.

"I've had to learn he isn't comfortable thinking and responding quickly out loud. That's my world, not his. A few times we got into a conflict and I pressured him so much he just let fly with an outburst that seemed extreme. I learned not to push. It's better to let him think first.

"I've also learned not to interrupt Frank with every thought that pops into my head. I'm finally learning to edit and pick times when I can have his attention. I know my thinking out loud used to bother him because he thought I meant every word of it. I just like to sort things out, and I don't care who knows it. So now I just warn him, 'I'm just thinking out loud again. You can relax, because I'm not going to rearrange all the furniture in the house today.'

"You know, I used to think that Frank's quietness and withdrawal at times was a passive-aggressive way of getting back at me. But it wasn't. God made Frank and me as unique individuals. I just didn't understand it. Twice this last month he actually did some thinking out loud with me, which was wonderful.

"I've also learned that when I encourage him to be who he is, I receive more of what I need too. That's a fringe benefit. The other day I knew he was frazzled, but I wanted to talk. Usually, I would have forced the discussion or tried to, but I remembered a couple of passages from Proverbs, 'Don't talk so much. You keep putting your foot in your mouth. Be sensible and turn off the flow!' (10:19, TLB). And, 'Self-control means controlling the tongue! A quick retort can ruin everything' (13:3, TLB).

"So I said, 'You look like you need some recouping time. Why don't you go read or do whatever and maybe we could talk a bit later?' And we did talk—quite a bit. And I am learning to write him notes too.

"Frank understands things that used to really get to me. He's better at communicating now, but I've learned that a few of his words mean a hundred of mine. When he gets a big smile on his face and doesn't say much, I say, 'It looks like that smile is about five hundred of my words.' And he says, 'You've got that right. I just love good translators!'

"So I've learned to give him time and space and not to interrupt when he talks. And I don't assume anymore that he doesn't have opinions or want to talk. He's selective and more methodical. I use a scatter-shot approach."[9]

The stories you heard were true. The people, well, I've heard this conversation so many times I've lost count. In this case, the results were positive. We had an introvert husband and an extrovert wife learning about the uniqueness of one another and discovering it is all right to be the way they are.

Keep in mind, when communicating, most women tend to focus more on others and men focus more on themselves. This helps to explain why women tend to expand topics whereas men like to shrink-wrap their presentation. Men like to keep it short and to the point. They also like to hear it this way.

Have you ever heard the following phrases from a man? (If you haven't, something is wrong!)

"I'm doing OK."

"It's fine."

"No problem."

"No big deal."

"I can handle it."

What's the message behind these statements? Is it "I'd love to talk more about this"? Not quite. It's just the opposite. It's his signal that he doesn't need to or want to discuss this any further because he will handle, solve, and take care of the situation.

Often a man has had a topic on the back burner, and it has simmered for a while, so when he's ready to communicate it's cooked and ready to serve. This is especially true if he's an introvert like Frank. He speaks when he's ready. Discussing it privately with himself inside his head helps him get ready to communicate. But too often his wife may interpret this as not being interested or attentive or as withdrawing from her. This may not be the case at all. You may want to ask if this is so and then encourage him to actually put it on the back burner.

A wife left her husband a note on a funny card which said, "Have I got a deal for you! Try and turn this one down. I like your conclusions, and I'd like them even more if you'd take a couple of minutes and tell me the process of how you arrive there. You know me. I'm just interested in how anything works. You can count on me working on being more bottom-line when I'm talking with you. How about it?" It worked.

Most women enjoy sharing and expanding their topic out loud. When a man starts talking, he usually knows where he's going unless he's an extrovert and just thinks out loud. But when many women begin talking, it's a discovery process. They're not always sure where it's heading and where it may end up. But thinking out loud helps them decide. Most men don't operate that way.

One wife shared, "I asked my husband whether he wanted me to do my out-loud thinking in front of him or outside in the garage. He looked at me kind of strange and said, 'Of course, I don't want you to go outside. I'll work at getting used to it. That stuff we heard on gender differences has helped me make sense of it too.'"

Sometimes an introvert husband is not always ready to give more than a yes or no response. So some women "rescue" the uncomfortable silence by filling in with their own words. It's better to say, "I'm interested in what you have to say, but you may need to think about it for a while. That's fine with me; take your time. When you're ready to talk about it, let me know." Giving permission for silence will take the pressure off both of you. It's also an encouragement to him.

Or, "The look on your face tells me that you have something on your mind. I'd like to hear what it is." Or, "You may be concerned about how I will respond if you share what's on your mind. I think I'm ready to listen." Or, "It appears that you're having difficulty speaking right now. Can you tell me why?" Or, "Perhaps your silence reflects a concern about saying something correctly. You can say it any way you'd like."

One wife said, "Sometimes when I want to talk with you, you seem preoccupied or hesitant. I wonder if it's the topic or if there is something I do that makes it difficult for you to respond. Maybe you could think about it and let me know later." Then she stood up and began to leave the room. But her quiet husband said, "Let's talk now. I'm ready to comment on your last statement."[10]

I've already mentioned the idea of learning to speak the man's language. (Remember, I encourage men to do the same, so this isn't a one-sided arrangement.)

Speaking your spouse's language includes not only vocabulary but also the person's packaging. Packaging refers to whether a person is an amplifier (sharing great volumes of details) or a condenser (sharing little more than the bottom line).

If he's an amplifier, go for it. If he's a condenser, keep it brief. Neither men nor women want to hear a monologue of the reasons why they need to fulfill a request.

Amplifiers give a number of descriptive sentences as they talk, while condensers give one or two sentences. In approximately 70 percent of marriages, the man is the condenser, and the woman is the amplifier. Neither is a negative trait, but the amplifier wishes his or her partner would share more, while the condenser wishes his or her partner would share less. It is only when each of you adapts to the style of your partner that real communication occurs.

Always, always talk about what you want and present it in such a way that your man catches in your request the belief that he can do it. Then he will be encouraged!

Chapter
4

Have you ever wanted to know what goes on
in the mind of a man for a day?

Chapter 4

Men Speak Out

Have you ever wanted to know what goes on in the mind of a man for a day? Would it help you understand them? You're probably saying yes to both questions. I've listened to other men for more than thirty years in the counseling office as well as conducted surveys nationally on various questions and issues. And in conducting these surveys, I discovered it was far easier to get women to respond than men!

In marriage conferences we've had the men sit in small groups with their wives seated right behind them listening to the men discuss assigned questions. After all the joking and wisecracks were over, it's amazing to hear the depth of their discussions. The wives (who incidentally couldn't say anything) were also amazed at what they learned.

In one survey each man was asked *indirectly* how he would like to be encouraged by his wife. The actual question was: What one thing would you like your wife to do that would indicate to you that she understands and accepts what you deal with in your daily life? (Some of these responses were shared in my book, *What Men Want*.)

"I would like my wife to show appreciation in recognizing the pressures we men go through and the responsibilities of being the provider and caretaker. Not only financially, but in the spiritual, emotional, social, and mental areas as well. As a man my concentration is on the overall picture and goals. It's true some of the attention to detail gets lost in the shuffle. But what I do is often misunderstood, and the appreciation for what I am doing gets lost."

"I want to feel needed and know I am important at home. I'm sensitive to not only what is said, but also how it's said. Criticism shuts me down. It would help if our wives who are full-time homemakers and haven't worked in the competitive, chaotic world outside of the home could understand that it is difficult and challenging for Christian men to interact and work under the constant influences of non-Christian attitudes all day."

"Do women really understand how we feel about the responsibility for making ends meet? Their actions tells us they don't. We feel burdened to provide for the family whether our wives are employed or not. Many of us fear disappointing the family and failing in our roles of protector, provider, father, family leader, and spiritual head. Our self-worth, our egos, and our identities are linked to both work and home. It often appears that we are not as interested in what goes on at home as we are with what happens at work. That may not always be the case—we may just be exhausted from work. It is frustrating for us not to have more time to give of ourselves at home."

Robert Lewis and William Hendricks in their book, *Rocking the Roles,* suggest that,

> First, your husband needs your support for his work. How you feel about his work is vitally important. Work is one way he has of defining himself. So how you feel about his work translates in his mind into how you feel about him. If you encourage and back him in his work, your support stabilizes and energizes him.
>
> But suppose you care little about what he does for a living; suppose you make no effort to even understand it; suppose you're interested only in what kind of money he makes; suppose you choose not to understand the pressure he's under; suppose you resent his work, or maybe even compete with him through your own career. Through any of these attitudes, you'll knock the props out from under your husband and stir up his insecurity. You'll leave him feeling empty, resentful, and confused.
>
> In his mammoth work *Seasons of a Man's Life*, Daniel Levinson found that men choose women to marry who they think will "nourish their life's vision" and help them fulfill their identity in a life work.[1] They desire wives who are behind them, encouraging them, supporting them, and cheering for them. If, after marriage, a wife fails to share in her husband's vision or participate in it, or if she becomes apathetic toward his work, or even resentful of it, then that marriage will fall into deep trouble within a surprisingly short time.
>
> For the record, I'm not saying that as a wife you should endorse your husband's workaholism. That's an unhealthy pattern, and I would never encourage a woman to enable that. But I want you to understand how important work is to the heart and soul of your man. How you stand behind his life's work is critical to his self-esteem.[2]

Right or wrong, good or bad, like it or not, a man does use his work to build his identity. He uses his work to express who he is just as a woman finds other ways to express who she is. Work also gives a man a purpose for his life, and for many it's satisfying. In their book, *Your Work Matters to God*, William Hendricks and Doug Sherman talk about biblical purposes for working. "Through work we serve people, through work we meet our own needs, through work we meet our families needs, through work we earn money to give to others, through work we love God."[3]

Hopefully these are the reasons the man in your life works! Listen carefully when he shares his concerns about his work.

Suggestion: Encourage your husband to make a list of the various pressures he faces or you make a list of potential work pressures and ask him to check off the main ones that apply to his job situation. Then ask how you can help. One wife asked to go to work with her husband for a day and just observe what he had to deal with. She told him beforehand she wouldn't make suggestions or comments unless he asked her to do so. It may help sometime to turn on a tape recorder at home to record an interchange. This has helped many discover whether what they say is constructive and supportive.

One man said, "I long to be appreciated for who I am, especially at home. I want to experience unconditional love at home—not just performance-based love. I struggle with that all day long on the job. When I come home, I don't always want to hear how hard my wife has worked. I need to hear some loving compliments, not just complaints! If I hear something uplifting first, I can problem-solve better."

Suggestion: One wife made a point of either telling or writing a note stating how much she appreciates what the man in her life accomplishes. A grateful daughter took the time to write her father a letter expressing appreciation for all he had done for her. If you're a wife you may want to practice the "Four Minute Drill" at the end of the day when you first see your husband. During the initial four minutes, make it a point to touch, hug, be affirming, friendly, and positive. Save the complaints about "his kids" and the broken plumbing until after he's eaten dinner. Remember, what takes place during the first four minutes when you see each other at the end of the workday sets the tone for the rest of the evening. If it's positive, it tends to continue in that direction. If it's negative . . . need I say more?

One man said: "I would love my wife to give me a hug, a kiss (without having to ask for one or be the initiator), and ask me to share what's going on in my head. And, after I'm done unloading all my concerns and worries not to offer advice, unless asked, but pray with me for God's guidance. This would help me release all my anxieties to God and provide a clean heart for my family."

Another said: "If she and I could sit down at the end of the day and review the highlights. To share what we really think without having her making judgments about the people I work with. It would be nice to have a sounding board, someone to just bounce ideas off of, without judging. I would value her honest opinion."

Suggestion: This man is looking for his wife to be a support. In a case like this, ask him how he wants you to pray for him in the morning before he goes to work, send him an e-mail, or leave a message on his beeper that you're praying for him. Too often phone or other messages to a man at work are, "I need your advice" or "Something needs fixing."

A forty-year-old said, "I think I am still a big kid at heart. I would like my wife to give me more encouragement regarding my business life and my home life. Maybe more "that-a-boys" or "thank yous" or "good jobs." I am at a level in my company where I don't get it at the office. I do get some appreciation at home, but that kid in me needs more."

Suggestion: Have you ever asked who his encouragers are at work? Or how he would like to be encouraged by others at work? Remember, too, if your husband is an extrovert, he's the kind who may think he's done a good job but won't really believe it until he's heard it from someone else. So, even if you've said it once that week, you may need to say it more. It may help to find out if he prefers to hear it privately or in front of others.

As one man put it: "I need continual affirmation that I am a good father/husband. I never had any training in being either one. I guess I need the acknowledgment that I am doing the best I can, even if I don't quite measure up to all desires and expectations. Please don't compare me to other fathers! I'm not them. We're all different and need some help. Give me physical affection and let me know you're glad you married me. Sometimes I worry about this."

Suggestion: It's easy to look around and compare what you don't have. It's very deflating to a man to be compared even in a joking way. Men have to live with comparisons and competition all of their lives. They don't want this from their wives. It's a personal affront to them. You could encourage your man if he feels lacking in some areas by saying, "You know, we all do the best we can with the limited knowledge that we have. I do appreciate that. Are you comfortable with what you know now or would you like to become even more proficient?"

"The thing I want her to do the minute I walk in the door," said one man, "is not to hit me with instantaneous decisions. But how would I feel if I had been with small children all day? Another possibility would be that she could give up some responsibilities to have more time for me. She often is still folding clothes through the ten o'clock news, after which we retire. Often I seem to be last on her list."

Suggestion: It's true! Many men feel they get the leftovers after the children. There are solutions though. Suggest these and give him a choice. Let him know you want alone time with him. This can happen if:

1. You hire a babysitter for an hour each evening.

2. You work out a plan together to simplify some of the tasks.
3. He could help with some of the tasks which would give you some free time.

"I'm like many men," one man admits, "I love to create and build. Yes, I'm the one who watches *Home Improvement*. I like to work on the house, the barbeque grill, the boat, the lawn. I enjoy serving my wife in this way but it sure would help if she would explain what she wants before I complete the project. It's disheartening and demotivating to have to make changes once the job is finished. I hate to hear, 'Oh, I wish we had done this instead' after the work is done."

Suggestion: Be sure you've clarified and decided exactly what you want done before he gets involved. Once a man gets started on a project, he's single-minded. It throws him when changes occur, and if he hears after the fact that you would have preferred something else, he will interpret it as a personal criticism that he blew it. He feels his efforts were not appreciated. Two men shared both their disappointments and their desires.

"Before my wife can do one thing to demonstrate understanding, encouragement, or acceptance of my struggles, she needs to *make time* to talk in order to discover what they are. I know that this is a priority that we must share together. However, I do feel like a lower priority in my wife's life (after the needs of the children, her church commitments, and time spent with her friends) than she is in mine. I guess if I had to request only one thing, I would like my wife to change her tone of voice when she speaks to me. Her predominant tone is critical, negative, and belittling."

"I guess encouragement would be to work at taking the 'log out of her own eye' so she could help me with mine. Then I could really trust her statements of understanding. I feel like I am working to get healthier, and as head of the family it should probably start with me—I'm glad it has anyway. I feel she has yet to really start, so it's harder for her to comprehend and understand. When I know myself better and when she's begun to understand me, then I feel her statements and support will mean more, and I will be able to trust and receive them with more confidence. Too often now I feel that what I share comes back to 'hit' me at a later date. I'm working to process that and deal with this issue with her. Not having to worry about when will I get hit with this again would be a relief and be encouraging as well."

Suggestion: This is a common issue between husbands and wives. To reiterate an earlier point, we are not trying to let men off the hook at all. They share in these problems quite often by not being available, not sharing, or by being defensive. You can't wait for the other person to change before you respond in new ways.

There are scriptural guidelines for the way you interact with the men in your life. There is a right time to speak and a time to be quiet. Proverbs 10:19 emphasizes this. "In a multitude of words transgression is not lacking, but he who restrains his lips is prudent."

The Living Bible is graphic in its rendering: "Don't talk so much. You keep putting your foot in your mouth. Be sensible and turn off the flow!"

"He who has knowledge spares his words, and a man of understanding has a cool spirit. Even a fool when he holds his peace is considered wise; when he closes his lips he is esteemed a man of understanding" (Proverbs 17:27–28).

"Do you see a man who is hasty in his words? There is more hope for a [self-confident] fool than of him" (Proverbs 29:20). Being hasty means blurting out what you are thinking without considering the effect it will have on others.

Romans 14:19 says, "So let us then definitely aim for and eagerly pursue what makes for harmony and for mutual upbuilding (edification and development) of one another." The word, *edify* which is part of helping, means to hold up or to promote growth in Christian wisdom, grace, virtue, and holiness.

A wife may correct what her husband says or does and tell him what to do and how to do something. But he probably won't respond well to her directions, especially if he does not feel admired. When a wife challenges, criticizes, or corrects her husband's decisions or initiations (especially in front of others), he feels unloved, angry, and humiliated. He wants to be encouraged to do things on his own. Instead, ask if he would like to hear an observation and if he doesn't, let it go. When a wife shares her displeasure by asking questions that carry an accusatory tone implying "You blew it," she can count on a defensive response.

Common defense-producing questions are "How could you?" or "Why in the world did you do that?" When questions are asked or statements made such as the following, a man will feel unaccepted, unapproved, and unloved, definitely not encouraged.

- "How can you think of buying that? You already have two and you rarely use them."

- "Those dishes are still wet. They'll dry streaked unless you redo them."

- "Your hair is getting kind of ragged, isn't it?"

- "There's a parking spot over there. Go over there and turn around quickly."

- "You shouldn't work so hard. None of the other men do."

- "Don't put that there. It will get lost."

- "You should call an electrician. He'll know what to do."

- "Why are we waiting for a table? Didn't you call ahead?"

- "You should spend more time with your sons. They miss you."

- "Your office is still a mess. How can you think in here? When are you going to clean it up?"

- "You forgot to bring it home again. Maybe you could write yourself a note."

- "You're driving too fast. Slow down."

- "Next time we should read the movie reviews; this wasn't good."

- "I didn't know what time to expect you. You should have called."

- "Somebody drank from the milk bottle again."

- "Don't eat with your fingers. You're setting a bad example for the kids."

These statements will elicit a response, but probably not the one you want.[4]

Share your concern in a calm voice, saying, "I am upset, and I don't want to be. Help me to understand what is happening. I need your perspective." This positive approach is more easily accepted than an accusation.

In a similar way a man said the following: "The one thing that I would like my wife to do is to encourage me. To create for me a place in her arms or in my home that is a shelter from the things I'm dealing with, not more demands or expectations. And not her personal suggestions of how I should deal with these things unless I solicit her opinion. Her encouragement would be in the form of words and actions. Words like: 'You're doing so well,' 'You can do it,' and 'I know what you do will be the best.' And actions like finding ways to lighten my load; or just saying OK and doing something I suggest. Just agreeing would be a form of encouragement. Encouraging me to be myself would indicate to me that she accepts me, rather than always trying to change me. Wanting me different means not accepting who I am."

Suggestion: A wife often tries to improve her husband's responses or help him by offering unsolicited advice. And strange as it seems when a woman offers unsolicited advice to a man, he tends not to see it as helpful but rather interprets it as, "You don't know what to do, and you need my help." If the man came from a home in which he was criticized as a child, he will activate those leftover responses to his present relationship. Even if they're not, men like to think of themselves as experts. It's the old desire to be proficient and in control. And if you suggest that he listen to the advice of an expert, he could really be upset.[5]

His response to you may be that he feels unloved because he feels you are not trusting him. You could say, "I've got a suggestion if you're interested. You let me know if you are."

Or a wife may try to change or control her husband's behavior by talking about how upset she is or letting him know her negative feelings. Again, his response is, "She doesn't love me because she doesn't accept me the way I am." Your requested change may be quite insightful, but it's not packaged in a way that is heard. Sharing the request in a positive way, pointing to the desired response, and even expressing it in writing often works better.

Do you find yourself noticing or acknowledging what your husband has done? Or instead do you comment on what has *not* been accomplished? That's discouraging and disheartening. Naturally, he feels unappreciated and taken for granted. Men and women want their *efforts* to be recognized and valued. Appreciation is the best way to see the desired behavior continue.

Men want to feel successful. They want to be successful in their male-female relationships. Too often they end up feeling like a failure, which is very discouraging. It's easy to give up and withdraw.

Here are some statements you can use to help a man communicate, to encourage him, but also to instruct him in a non-threatening way.

- "I really feel safe when I share my feelings with you."

- "It really helps me solve problems and fix things when you listen to me."

- "I appreciate how you help me arrive at my own solutions to some of my problems!"

- "I really feel affirmed by you when you see my opinion as having validity. Sometimes I really need your perspective."

- "I like it when you let me problem-solve out loud and find the solution. I know you have some good ideas and holding them back must be hard at times."

- "I want to take three minutes and tell you what happened. I think you'll find these details interesting and pertinent to this incident."

One of the statements *not* to make is, "You don't understand." This not only discourages a man but frustrates him. He then tends to tune out whatever your explanation is going to be. If he doesn't catch what you've said you could say, "Let me put it another way." Then be sure to put it in his language and keep it brief.[6]

Another man said he wished his wife would, "Defend me . . .

not in a way that says I'm always right, but in a way that indicates she knows I'm really trying . . . there is a lot of criticism of men in today's society . . . I want to know my wife is on my side, not on the side that is critical. And I must say, I believe she is and does. For that I am grateful."

Suggestion: Making the statement, "I believe in you" or putting a note in your husband's pocket can be helpful. Watch the questions you ask because a man may think you're being judgmental. Preface your questioning with, "I want to understand what you're experiencing. That's why I'm asking these questions."

"One of the ways I feel affirmed is sex," says one man. "I like sex and I need it. Sex is on men's minds a lot. On our own we think about it. Also, we are constantly barraged with sexual temptation in the media, from newspaper ads to films. They hit us at our weakest point. The guy who says he never notices is either lying or a walking cadaver."

Still other men say, "Our eyes are the problem. Men have innate visual scanners for anything that appeals sexually. Don't think we don't notice. The old adage that 'Women have to be in the mood, and men have to be in the room' is true. Resistance is a struggle for Christian men."

"There is also a strong connection between a man's sex drive and his ego. Women need to know how they impact us. The way they dress, wiggle, look, or touch us affects us. We struggle constantly with keeping our sex lives pure, especially when our wives are cold. Sometimes we don't want to be romantic—we just want to have sex. Other times we need to know we are desired, loved, and accepted. We enjoy having our wives take the initiative."

Suggestion: Be as attractive as possible, initiate and discuss what, how, and when!

Three men in a small group were asked what their wives could do to encourage them. They were quite specific in what they said.

"I would love for my wife to ask questions that would lead to a greater understanding of who I am and what I have to deal with daily. I believe this would lead to a greater appreciation of me."

"Just to have her assure me that she will support and love me no matter what happens. Even if I lose my job or am uncertain about what to do next with my life. To affirm that God is in control and she is trusting Him to care for both of us."

"Women like to vent their feelings to a listening spouse without editorials or comments. I would like my wife to draw out my feelings about a situation but never editorialize or attempt to define what I mean. Next Tuesday evening after thinking about a specific situation, I may change my mind 180 degrees. I would like to be allowed to mull over things without being thought of as rude or disinterested."[7]

I asked this specific question of a group of men, "What could your wife do that would encourage you more?" Here are a few of the responses I received.

"It would be nice if she would initiate lovemaking from time to time. However, the mitigating circumstances are our three sons ages five, four, and two. She has little energy left over most days."

———

"I would love for her to be more consistent in assisting me with the everyday details that make up our days, such as dinner, laundry, housecleaning, and paying bills. Through these helps, she encourages me that I'm not alone."

———

"It would be encouraging to me if she would comment on the things that I do as favors because I am wanting to help out. She tends to see my efforts to help as obligations that I should be doing anyway.

"But, I would like my wife to encourage me when I am down, distraught, overwhelmed, and beaten. I don't need her advice nor any sympathy, I just need to hear her gently say to me, 'Honey, I know you are hurting. I may not be able to help you solve your problem, but tell me what is bothering you. And let's ask the Father to help you and to comfort you.' And most of all, give me time to 'brew over it.'"

———

"I want her to be more encouraging and truly desirous of giving encouragement rather than focusing on her own difficulties. And to be more encouraging in the sense that she's on my side rather than being adversarial, putting me on the defensive by saying, 'Why didn't you say. . . ?' or, 'Why did you do that?'

"By avoiding reminding me that something should be obvious to me and why did I bring it up. By being more mindful of my need for touching or a hug, even if it's not obvious that I need it. By being more receptive and grateful for even the small things that I do to let her know I am thinking of her."

In a national survey which included more than three hundred men of all ages, this is what they said in response to the statement, "I would appreciate it if my partner would . . ." The items which received the highest responses of important or very important were the following. You may be surprised by some of the findings.

Ninety to 100 percent of the men said listening to their ideas and being fun to be around were at the top of the list.

Listening was a top priority. Eighty to 90 percent wanted their wives to listen to their concerns, verbally say "I love you," show appreciation for what their husbands do for them, show independence, and pursue their own interests.[8]

There is one last subject that is a source of tension, controversy, and difference between men and women. Men have strong concerns about this issue which is—their feelings.

⌒

"We're always taking hits about emotions, feelings, or whatever you call them. There is confusion here for both men and women. We are emotional beings. We are not as insensitive as we are stereotyped to be, but we have difficulty moving from the logical/linear side of the mind to the emotional if we are left-brained males. Not all of us are left-brained either."

⌒

"Stereotypes limit us. Women are convinced that all men think about is power and sex, or sex and power! So when we do open up emotionally, our response is automatically classified as one of these areas."

⌒

"I would say many women don't understand the reality and depth of emotional pain men feel, especially when it is related to feelings of inadequacy imposed by society's markings of a real man—financial success, sexual potency, physical stature, competency, etc. I wonder if the average wife knows how much her husband needs her support, admiration, and affirmation."

⌒

"My wife says things to me that hurt deeply. She says them in passing without much emotion or anger, just off the cuff. She seems to say them at times when discussion would be inappropriate (i.e., when other people are present). Finally when we do get time to talk, the hurt is less severe or I just let it pass. This is probably more my problem than hers."

⌒

"We struggle with emotions and stress. It seems that women, even those from the feminist groups, feel that they have all the stress. I don't know if they understand the gigantic responsibility we face being God's umbrella of protection for our families in a world that has such great negative influence and unhealthy attractions. It is hard to keep all your ducks in a straight line at times.[9]

Remember that when a man does share his feelings with you, it's often difficult for him. It's also a big step because most men haven't learned a feeling vocabulary nor are they adept at giving word pictures. It would be helpful to him if you recognized his attempts and his progress. When feelings are shared he does not want to hear judgments or criticisms. Remember that the way he shares as well as the amount of sharing he does will probably not be the same way you share. That's all right. You're not to be his instructor at this time.

He may stop to think about what he wants to say. Don't fill in the silent times. In your heart and mind give him all the time he needs to formulate what is occurring within him.

Since it is a step in vulnerability to share his feelings with you, keep what is said in confidence. Let him know you will do this. He doesn't want your mother, his mother, or your friends to know.

When feelings are shared he may be simply stating them, not offering them up for discussion. Either let him lead in this or ask if he wants you to just listen or respond.

When you want to know what he is feeling ask, "What's your reaction to this?" rather than, "What are you feeling?" He can respond best to the first question.

Never, but never, interrupt. I remember the first occasion I shared with my wife, Joyce, about the times when I had been depressed. I sat at the dining area table and Joyce stood thirty feet away with her back to me washing the dishes. When I started sharing, she stopped what she was doing, came over, sat down, and listened. Never once did she interrupt or make a value judgment on what I was sharing. I felt safe.

Interruptions cause men to retreat and think, *Why bother sharing?* Always remember, sharing feelings takes more effort, energy, and concentration for men than it does for women. Men need to stay focused on one thing at a time. Interruptions throw them off course; and because they are goal conscious, they like to stay on course and complete the process.

Distractions make it difficult for a man to sort through the time-consuming process of interpreting his emotions. Many men are not emotionally articulate because they lack language skills in this area. When you are patient and accept this lack, it helps him talk more.

A wife shared with me a commitment note she gave her husband. She said it brought about the emotional interchange she had wanted for years. The note read, "Since sharing your emotions with me is such a cherished experience and so vital to a wonderful sexual relationship, I commit myself to you to respond in the following manner: When you share, you can count on me to listen, not expect you to describe your feelings exactly as I do, not interrupt, nor make value judgments. And finally, if we do enter into a discussion, I will limit my participation to fifteen minutes." Her husband was very encouraged!

Two days later she received a dozen roses and a note that said, "Thank you," and then, "My commitment when you share is 'ditto.' I won't try to solve the problem unless you ask me to!"

You may look at the man in your life and see power, strength, and determination. You may think, *Why does he need encouragement? He's got it all together. He's secure.*

Years ago a handwritten note was passed from teacher to teacher. I think it describes all of us as men.

⁓

Don't be fooled by me. Don't be fooled by the mask I wear. For I wear a mask. I wear a thousand masks. Masks that I'm afraid to take off, and none of them are me. Pretending is an art that is second nature with me, but don't be fooled. I give the impression that I'm secure, that all is sunny and unruffled with me, that the waters are calm, and that I'm in command, and I need no one. But don't believe it. Please don't. My surface may seem smooth, but my surface is my mask. Beneath lays no smugness. Beneath dwells the real me, in confusion, in fear, in loneliness. But I hide this. I don't want anybody to know it.

I panic at the thought of my weakness being exposed.

That's why I create a mask to hide behind, to help me pretend. To shield me from the glance that knows. I'm afraid your glance will not be followed by love and acceptance, I'm afraid that you'll think less of me, that you'll laugh, and that your laugh will kill me. I'm afraid that deep down inside I'm nothing. That I'm just no good, and that you'll see and reject me.

So I play my games, my desperate pretending games, with the facade of assurance on the outside and a trembling child within. And so my life becomes a front. I idly chatter with you in the suave tones of surface talk, I tell you everything that's really nothing. Nothing of what's crying within me. So when I'm going through my routine, don't be fooled by what I'm saying. Please listen carefully, and try to hear what I am not saying, what I would like to be able to say. What for survival I need to say, but I can't say. I dislike the hiding. Honestly I do. I dislike the superficial phony games I'm playing. I'd really like to be genuine, spontaneous, and me.

Can you help me? Help me by holding out your hand, even when that's the last thing I seem to want or need. Each time you're kind and gentle and encouraging, each time you try to understand because you really care, my heart begins to grow wings, very small wings, very feeble wings, but wings. With your sensitivity and sympathy, and your power of understanding, I can make it. You can breathe life into me. It will not be easy. A long conviction of worthlessness builds strong walls. But love is stronger than strong walls, and therein lies my hope.

Please try to take down those walls with firm hands, but with gentle hands. For a child is very sensitive, and I am a child. Who am I you may wonder? I am someone you know very well. I am every man you meet.[10]

Chapter 5

*Sometimes in an attempt to be an encourager,
you end up crossing the line and
become a pleaser.*

Chapter 5

What *Not* to Do—or the Worst Mistakes You Could Make

"Norm, are there limits to encouragement? After all, you don't know my husband. Let me tell you about him. He's . . ."

"Norm, does encouraging him mean I sell out? Do I become a nothing trying to meet his needs all the time? What about . . ."

"Norm, what if . . ?"

"Norm, what about . . ?"

The questions are endless. But they're good honest questions. Hopefully there will be some answers!

Sometimes in an attempt to be an encourager, you end up crossing the line and become a pleaser. But that's not the only line that can be crossed. We need to consider the worst things you could do for you and for him. In this chapter, we'll look at problem behaviors which plague many marriages. Space does not permit discussing the background and reasons for these behaviors. Instead we'll focus on some suggestions as to what you can do.

Avoid becoming a controller in your relationship and also avoid letting yourself be controlled. Sometimes one partner ends up being smothered by the other. Allowing this to happen is no way

93

to encourage someone! If you end up letting the other person control you, the result is you end up feeling unnecessary. Total dependence on another is not the way Christ has called us to live. Jesus has called us to equality, not domination. Jesus has called us to willingly serve one another, not just one to serve the other.

From the passage in Ephesians 5:22–31 and from the creation account, it's possible to discover what a husband needs from his wife. As we look at the early chapters of Genesis we see he needs a woman of strength, a helper who will respond to his leadership as he sets out to subdue and populate the earth. Nancy Groom in her book *Married without Masks* states,

> Adam (even after the Fall) would have been disappointed if Eve had refused to engage with him as his partner in the work God had called both of them to do. He did not need a slave; he needed a woman who knew who she was and was confident in her gifts. An alive, vibrant woman gives zest and excitement to her husband's life. He needs that.[1]

Remember this fact: One of the main causes for the death of love on the part of one person for another is when their partner controls and dominates them. (See chapter 2 of my book *Secrets of a Lasting Marriage*.)

Look at what God's Word says: "For all of you who were baptized into Christ have clothed yourselves with Christ. There is neither Jew nor Greek, there is neither slave nor free man, there is neither male nor female; for you are all one in Christ Jesus" (Galatians 3:27–28, NASB).

What our world sees as a leadership model goes counter to what Jesus has said: "But Jesus called them to Himself, and said, 'You know that the rulers of the Gentiles lord it over them, and their great men exercise authority over them. It is not so among you, but whoever wishes to become great among you shall be your servant, and whoever wishes to be first among you shall be your slave; just as the Son of Man did not come to be served, but to serve, and to give His life a ransom for many'" (Matthew 20:25–28, NASB).

Servanthood is the model of leadership that Jesus is teaching. Remember that the only way that you can really encourage another person in a healthy way is to be sure that you encourage yourself. And you can do this because of knowing who you are in Jesus Christ.

The best way to be healthy as well as to be an encourager in a relationship is to be healthily independent or *interdependent*. The person whose identity is found through others often ends up with relationships that are addictive.

Dependency in relationships is not a Christian calling except for being dependent upon God, which all men and women are called to be.

An *independent* woman thrives on individuality, few restrictions, and self-gratification. She finds her identity through herself.

But there is a third option called *interdependence*. The interdependent woman has a strong sense of personhood and bases this upon being affirmed by God. She knows she has been given gifts and is willing to use them, but she can also rely upon others. This woman views others as her equal and also values herself. Are you a dependent, independent, or interdependent woman?

In *Free to Be God's Woman,* Jan Congo gives four options in which to view ourselves and others. A *dependent* woman says, "I am nothing and you are nothing," or "I am nothing but you are a person of worth and dignity." The *independent* woman says, "I am a person of worth and dignity but you are expendable." The *interdependent* woman says, "I am a person of worth and dignity, and you are a person of worth and dignity."

In this last option, competition does not exist. Competition between women and between men and women is a reflection of insecurity.

The interdependent woman allows herself and others the freedom to grow and be in process. She has role flexibility. She is relying on God's expectations for herself rather than others.

This style of living neither intimidates knowingly nor is intimidated. The interdependent woman does not try to prove she is superior to others nor does she attempt to live the way the world values people.

One final thought: An interdependent woman has balance in her relationships. She enters into relationships with others but she does not restrict them nor is she responsible for them. She discovers the value of commitment.[2]

This is best summarized by Jan Congo:

> Now we, as Christ's followers, find ourselves growing through healthy relationships. In 1 John 4:12 (NASB) it says, "No one has beheld God at any time; if we love one another, God abides in us, and His love is perfected in us." The Christian life was not meant to be lived in a vacuum. We are encouraged to be involved in relationships.
>
> As we rub shoulders with each other we see the need to be committed to one another. Only in commitment to imperfect human beings can we follow in our Master's footsteps.
>
> The very word *commitment* grinds on many eardrums today in this independent, self-centered society of ours. Yet it is only after we have committed ourselves to the God of love that we can commit ourselves to care for others and identify with them in their various stages of growth. We refuse to make others either our projects or our heroes. Instead we choose to walk, as much as is humanly possible, where they have walked, to laugh and weep with them, to be available to them, to be as gentle with them as Jesus Christ is with us and to be vulnerable to them, demonstrated by our willingness to speak the truth in love about

ourselves when we are with them. I choose to back up my words with an authentic lifestyle. In relationships I am willing not only to give but also to express my needs honestly and receive from others.

We are one of the best means of getting God's life and love to others. Jesus is our source of strength so never do we purposely choose to have others become dependent on us. In all of our relating, we must remember that the purpose is for Christ to be formed in you and in me (Gal. 4:19). If we find ourselves imitating anyone but Christ or pressuring someone else to imitate us then we need to confess and readjust. We need to honestly share, with no inhibitions, what we see happening and together we need to get our friendship back to its original purpose—that Christ will be formed in both of us.

Love is the evidence that I am Christ's woman. Only through dependence on Christ alone will I find myself freed to be a most courageous lover who will not lose her identity through loving but will find her God-given purpose in loving.[3]

Encouraging a husband does *not* mean that you become so absorbed in your husband that your identity and value come from him. It's *not* becoming a doormat with no ideas, opinions, or voice, nor does it mean becoming an appeasing woman. Encouragement is not manipulation either. It's not done for the purpose of reshaping him for your own dreams, desires, or wishes. Absorption, appeasement, and manipulation are actually forms of control.

Do you realize that if you cooperate with a controller you're encouraging him? That's right, you're encouraging him . . . to continue to control! If you happen to be in this situation, here are some phrases you can use which will encourage him to respond in a healthier way. Remember that your tone of voice and nonverbals have much to say as well.

- "When you remind me to put the magazines in the rack when I leave the room, I really feel bothered and hovered over. Please wait until I'm through reading for that time period and I will put them away. I do understand how important this is to you."

- "When you tell me how much lipstick to wear, I don't feel accepted. I feel like you're trying to make me over so I won't embarrass you. I would like you to let me be me and decide how I would like to groom myself. If you do this I will feel more positive toward you. And I think you will like the result."

- When you continue to check the way I'm cooking the meal, I feel like a child. I feel like my abilities are being evaluated by someone who is not an expert, and it irritates me. Please let me do my job the way I do it. Then if you don't like the end result, we can discuss it to see what can be done, all right?"

Notice the formula in the above examples: You share your feelings, identify the unacceptable behavior, follow with a request, and then share what your husband will gain by responding to what you've said. It may help to identify the consequences if your request is unheeded. Some will be obvious, but it may help to clarify the natural consequences. And you need to be willing to follow through.

How do responses like this encourage? They promote a balanced relationship and you no longer participate in the control issue.

Avoid mothering the man in your life. Let me say it another way. *Never, but never mother a man.* When you act like a mother you can't encourage him. Treating an adult like a child is demeaning and makes you a controller! And if you mother him he will continue to act in a way that makes you continue to want to mother him and on and on and on.

How do mothers sound? Well for one thing they remind. They actually make the other person (child or adult) rely on them to bail them out. Anyway, why should the other person stop forgetting when he has someone who will remind him? Have you ever made statements like these?

- "Honey, be sure you've got your wallet."

- "Don't forget to stop and pick up some milk and butter on the way home."

- "Jim, don't you ever look at the gas gauge? You know how many times you've run out!"

- "Be sure to take a coat with you; you usually get cold."

- "John, if I've asked you once I've asked you a hundred times . . ."

- "You didn't call for the plane tickets. I'll do it for you . . . again."

You may be thinking, *What's wrong with those statements and questions? Aren't they just helpful reminders?* Perhaps. Once may be helpful, but too often these are repetitive. If you have to repeat them again and again, why keep on? It's obvious they're not working. They're what I call bail-out responses. They take the responsibility away from the other person. These statements say, "You're a child; you can't remember anything. I'll do it for you."

What is it that you remind and have been reminding your husband or son of for some time? I assume you remind so that he learns to remember by himself and so you won't have to remind anymore.

Similar to reminding is another approach. It's called rescuing. Years ago there was a song out with the title, "Rescue Me." If a man in your life sings this, don't listen.

How do you know if someone plays the role of a rescuee if you tend to be a rescuer? Think about these factors. Would that man be incapable of functioning in his daily life without your help? If so, don't rescue. Encourage growth.

Do you tend to be stronger than him? If so, don't reinforce his weaknesses and foster dependency. Find his potential and encourage growth.

Does he tend to be unhappy unless you're doing something for him? If so, don't play this game. Encourage by showing you believe in his capability to do it himself.

Does he make excuses for himself or do you make excuses for him? Remember excuses cripple and perpetuate helplessness.

But aren't you to love another person by helping and serving? Yes, but it can become rescuing when you believe that it's your responsibility to solve his problems or protect him from the results of what he's done.

Rescuing doesn't work. It doesn't promote growth or change. It doesn't help your man grow.

Sometimes women gain fulfillment by being a rescuer. It makes them feel good and look good in the eyes of others. The downside is you could end up with anger, resentment, feeling exhausted, or even demeaned.

Rescuing puts you in a position of control or power. It keeps others from focusing on your mistakes or problems. After all, who are they to talk!

Rescuing is a great diversion. You don't have to deal with your own issues if you're busy saving others.

It also doesn't make for much of an equal relationship or mutual submission as Scripture states (see Ephesians 5).

Rescuing is another word for fixing. Loving encouragement means support, being available, cooperative, and sympathetic.[4]

There are several ways you can mother a man if you really want to. You can do things for him that he could and should be doing for himself. This is a good way to keep him responding as a child.

You may find yourself caught up in playing "Twenty Questions" with him trying to find out what he wants, doesn't want, is or isn't thinking, etc. Guessing games to get information are just that—games. They belong with kids, not adults.

Mothering involves making assumptions that your man is going to commit the worst of all sins—forget or be absent-minded. This isn't encouraging; it's discouraging and reinforces his tendency to do what you don't want!

It's also a violation of 1 Corinthians 13. Love gives the other person the benefit of the doubt.

Close to this is taking charge of events or activities you think he's going to mess up. It lets him off the hook and helps him continue to be irresponsible.

By the way, you will get results with these approaches. He will probably begin to generate some anger which will breed resentment and could even turn into passive or out-and-out rebellion. That's just one possibility. I know you don't want that to happen!

He's not going to feel so good about himself because he's going to feel less than competent. And he may blame you which is a big turn off for him. And the end result is his romantic interest in you could diminish greatly. When resentment exists it's hard for romance to stay around. And in time the original love feelings could disappear as well.

What options do you have? Actually, several and they're positive for both of you. When you follow through with these you're sending the message, "I believe in you. I believe in your capability to be responsible, mature, and an adult!"

Actually the solutions are quite obvious. You will need to change your way of responding regardless of how you feel, what you've thought, and how you've responded. Has what you've been doing worked? No? Do you have much to lose with a new response? No? So go for it.

First, don't do anything more for your man that he *should be* (meaning capable of) doing for himself. If he asks you for something, and you're used to getting it for him, let him get it for himself. Don't make suggestions. Don't pick up after him. Don't bail him out of experiencing consequences. Yes, it probably means that your life could be a bit more frustrating. But you need to stick to your commitment. If you hear complaints let him know you know he's capable of assuming the responsibility himself. You may be the first person in his life to show a belief that he can be different. Treat him as though he is reliable. I've seen so many women who end up being the clock, calendar, key finder, garbage reinforcer, and appointment regulator. Don't rescue! Don't bail him out!

In counseling I've dealt with men like this. As we discuss together the situation the dialogue goes something like this:

Norm: John, you have a fairly responsible job, don't you?

John: Yes, I do. I've been there three years now.

Norm: And you've received a couple of promotions, haven't you?

John: Yes, one just recently.

Norm: John, when you're at work who is it that reminds you of what to do, when to do it, how to do your job?

John: Well, no one. I can handle all that myself. I don't need reminders.

> *Norm:* So you don't need any kind of reminders or support like that at work?
>
> *John:* No.
>
> *Norm:* I guess my question is, what's the difference?
>
> *John:* What's the difference?
>
> *Norm:* Yes, why are you so different at work? You're competent, reliable, functional, and you follow through. At home you're just the opposite. It appears that you're making a choice. You have the capability, and you choose to be that way at work. At home you have the same capability, but choose not to use it at home. I wonder what kind of message you're sending to your wife?

If a man is functional at work and not at home, there's some kind of game playing going on that needs to be exposed and stopped.[5]

Listen to the story of Eric and Jane as told by James Walker in his book *Husbands Who Won't Lead and Wives Who Won't Follow:*

> For a wife who has grown accustomed to it, refusing to "mother" can be painful. Some women may be faced with the disturbing thought that perhaps this role was exactly what they wanted in marriage. They saw the escapist's irresponsible tendencies, and they felt right at home with the prospect. The challenge of taking someone and remaking him might have been an equally compelling reason. Whatever the rationale, the notion of now opposing this lifestyle by doing nothing goes against all of her natural instincts, including her maternal desires.
>
> Eric's habit patterns included giving no help around the house. To Jane it was a constant source of irritation. He sat

watching TV while she asked, "Could you take out the garbage?" Her second, third, and fourth requests were always fended off with his desire to wait for a commercial, to finish the article he was reading, or the excuse that he had to wait till morning when he could see.

When she'd finally had enough, Jane agreed to begin some passive resistance. She asked Eric the familiar question, "Would you take out the garbage?" She asked only once. Thereafter, she began filling paper sacks beside the overflowing garbage can. The children noticed their shrinking kitchen, but it took Eric five days and walking into the pile on his way to the refrigerator between commercials to bring up the subject.

Jane's reaction was a calm one: "I asked you to take that out the other day. I knew you'd get to it whenever you were able." It was a polite but firm reply that communicated esteem for Eric and a new line that she would not cross. There are easier ways to handle a garbage problem. But Eric and Jane's problem was not garbage; it was irresponsibility.

Jane found pleasure in controlling her emotions by refusing to become angry. She also noticed a new delight in not allowing her emotions to be dictated by her husband. Her confidence grew to the point that she told Eric, "Sweetheart, you can notice when the garbage is full. From now on, I'll just let you decide when to take it out." Basically, Jane had to decide what she could live with—an overflowing trash can, or a growing anger and resentment toward her husband.

The difficult area for Jane was the checkbook. When they both agreed on a budget, it was decided that Eric would pay the bills. She got a check each week for groceries and her areas of management, i.e., clothes for her and the kids, school supplies, and household expenses.

Jane knew it was only a matter of time before things would bog down financially.

Several months later, as Eric looked for socks among the discards scattered across the top of his desk, he noticed and dug through the overdue bills piled around the "IN" box—just where he and Jane had agreed they would be placed. Frantically, he ripped them open to survey the damage. Each one was more devastating than the last. They were like cold buckets of water on a groggy morning. As he came down the stairs to find Jane, he felt angry and inwardly frightened.

Jane tried not to blink as he screamed into her face. She calmly looked into his eyes and said, "You agreed to be in charge of our finances, sweetheart. I did put the bills where you told me."

"Why didn't you open them and tell me about them?" he shouted.

"I just thought of them as your mail and I had confidence in you that you'd take care of them," she responded.

Later, as a much calmer Eric talked to me, he reassembled his thoughts. "I knew that all my life I just tried to get by. I didn't think of myself as lazy, but I suppose I was. I know I wasn't God's prize husband. Jane deserved better. But that day it hit me. Things weren't going to get any better if I didn't change."

What Jane had been trying to get across to Eric for twelve years, the garbage can and the bill collectors had managed to perform in three months![6]

Sometimes a man may not act capable because of other reasons such as the fear of failure.

When a man fails in one area, he will take on only "safe" tasks. Why should he attempt something that carried with it the uncertainty of risk? Therefore, some men will pull back from activities over which they don't maintain a high degree of control or in which they aren't certain of success.

This happened with Tom when he lost his job. Though he did not admit it at first, it was a terrible defeat.

Tom was also a good auto mechanic. He had an aged car that he tinkered with as a hobby. With a cavalier attitude, he told Cindy, his wife, "Now I've got the chance to put that old convertible back on the road. I'll look for a job when I'm ready. So don't bug me about it."

Tom told his friends he had enough money saved so that he could take his time to pick the job he wanted. He even bragged that he might make so much money on the sale of that old car that he could start working for himself. In point of fact, he was spending more cash for parts than their situation allowed, and he knew he was only staying busy enough to allow himself the luxury of not thinking.

Only later did Tom admit he was really afraid of being turned down for a new job. He deeply feared that his own incompetence or personality had cost him his former position, and he had no desire to suffer through a series of job-interview rejections.

The more Cindy expressed fears for their future, the more Tom heard one theme loud and clear: "You're not providing for us, and you're a failure." Cindy never said it, but Tom heard it. When Cindy initiated prayer, urged Tom in Bible reading or some area of spiritual leadership, he only saw her dissatisfaction with him. Whenever he entered the house and heard Cindy talking on the phone to a friend from church, he could tell by the hushed tone of her voice that he was the subject of conversation. He dreaded the glances of her friends at church and was embarrassed when the pastor inquired if they needed help. Therefore, he continued to lose himself in car grease, matinee movies, and Monday Night Football.

To compound his inner doubts, Tom began to see that his circumstances were putting him in the same place as his own father, a man who had never held a steady job for long. That notion horrified and angered him. He had no desire to live a life where he lacked respect. Tom became suspended between the fear of being a second-class citizen in his own home and his need to avoid the risk of further failure.

It was only after Cindy began the process of expressing her trust in Tom again and the belief that he would do the right thing that he began to see his home as a place where he could be safe. Home for Tom became a location where he could be understood and an avenue where he could risk failure and still not be devastated.

Each day Cindy's smile told him she believed in him and simply chose to ignore his failures. With that encouragement, Tom's inner motivation grew. Cindy's attitude toward her husband was not one that came from a downtrodden self-image but one that was a deliberate choice on her part. Again it was encouragement which made the difference.[7]

A wife shared with me how she was able to help and encourage her husband. "My husband had no conception of organization. He's a perfectionist and if something couldn't be done perfectly then he wouldn't do it at all, or he'd leave a job half complete. Needless to say, we had a lot of half-finished projects, a lot of messes, and a lot of tasks never started!

"I'm not a nag and I didn't pester him about the unfinished projects, but I did pick up the tools and materials left lying around and put them in big piles. I also have a drawer (big drawer) in the kitchen that I called his tool drawer. Anything I found lying around I put into that drawer. That way if anything was missing, he could find it either in a pile or in the drawer.

"This caused a lot of arguments because he said it was his house, too, and he should be able to have his items wherever he wanted. (My husband is a carpenter and some of these items included big boards on which he would write notes or phone numbers or lists of materials needed. I started burning the boards in the fireplace.) All this was after many requests for him to write on tablets and put things away.

"I started buying him organizational tools—a small handheld computer and tablets—and we worked on writing lists of things he needed to accomplish in a day. He prioritized the list. If he didn't have the materials needed to start a job, then it went to the bottom of the list.

"I showed him it was OK to do a job as good as you could; it didn't have to be perfect, and it didn't have to be better than any-one else could do it. He began to feel good about starting something, completing it, and crossing it off his list.

"I praised him when he began a job, during the job, and of course after it was complete he got lots of praise. Most of the time the finished project was better than anyone else could have done it.

"Praise was very important to him and I found he needed to hear me praise him to other people. I would tell the person what his next project was going to be and how excited I was about his plans. I guess he just needed a system to get him organized. He could see that if he didn't get organized his stuff was going to get burned or he was going to have a pile in the backyard as big as the house. He needed to know his projects were appreciated and we didn't expect perfection."

In any kind of encouragement be sure you don't fall into the trap of giving up your ministries, hobbies, or interests because they're not important to your man. Sometimes these changes occur so gradually, you're not even aware that you've made them.

This isn't healthy for you or for him. What's important to you doesn't have to have the same level of importance to him. You both need to encourage each other's uniqueness. The more you give up who you are, the less you care about yourself. This will tend to build up anger or resentment and you will be less likely to want to encourage.

I'd like to come back to another concern that's mentioned elsewhere in this book. If you don't feel good about yourself or if you don't encourage yourself, you will have difficulty honestly and genuinely encouraging the significant man in your life. How do you see yourself?

There's another trap that women fall into that may even sound scriptural, "I must decrease so he can increase." That's not what the Bible says. But some highly gifted and competent women feel that in order to build up and encourage a man they need to hold back their abilities and giftedness because if they expressed who they really were their man would feel insecure. I hope my response to that doesn't sound too harsh but, if he does, it's not your fault. It's his problem. Your strengths and giftedness are from God. They're not meant to be thwarted by anyone.

You may say, "I don't hold back or cover up." But sometimes women do and they aren't even aware of it. For example, do you put yourself down, make derogatory comments about yourself or call attention to any mistakes you make in front of your husband? Do you brush aside his compliments or argue about them to prove he shouldn't have a positive opinion of you? Do you put a lid on your abilities so that the attention usually is directed to him?

All of these are telltale signs.[8]

This is not the way you were called to live.

Chapter
6

The average man sees sex as the main way to be close to his wife.

Chapter 6

Encouraging Your Husband through Sex and Romance

"Encouraging him sexually! What man needs any encouragement there? His 'on' button is never 'off'!"

"I don't think that's an area I can do much about. The sex is there, but romance is what's needed. I'm not sure how to encourage him romantically."

Is sex all men ever think about? Well, they do think about it . . . a lot. Sexual thoughts flit in and out of a man's mind all day long. Men think about, dream about, and daydream about sex far more than you probably ever realized. Even though men slow down in their thoughts about sex when they're in their forties and fifties, they still think about it several times a day. Men tend to dream about sex three times as often as women. Their performance orientation to life flows into the sexual areas as well, and their greatest fear is the "I" word—impotence. The average man sees sex as the main way to be close to his wife. Archibald Hart describes it well:

> Sure, the average man thinks of other things, like football and politics, but eventually all mental roads lead back to

this one central fixation: Sex. There are times when the obsession fades and even vanishes. Give him a golf bag or a fishing trip. He'll forget about sex for a while. But sooner or later, like a smoldering fire, it will flare up again. Strong, urgent, forceful, and impatient, the sex drive dominates the mind and body of every healthy male. Like it or not, that's the way it is.[1]

Men want sex for a number of reasons including physical release, giving or receiving comfort, affection and encouragement, love, proving one's popularity, masculinity, or sexual ability, and expressing tenderness.

One husband said, "I guess sex means many things to me. Sometimes I'm romantic and that's the reason. I want to be close. Other times I'm down and sex is comforting. Sometimes I just want a quick release."

The sexual relationship could be the primary means a husband uses to feel connected to his wife. It can be a time of special closeness for them both.

We live in a sexually-oriented society. We talk a lot about sex but we really don't talk about sex. Contradictory? No. You probably know what I mean. Most couples don't have serious indepth talks about sex and romance. It just happens. They do it. It may be fulfilling and then again, it may not. It's a vital part of married life and can be so enriching for both husband and wife.

Let's face it. Sex is at the top of the list for men. They struggle with it. Too often they think of just their own needs. Men won't like this statement, but most men are not as knowledgeable about sex as they think they are! We as men have a lot to learn about lovemaking. And believe it or not, women can help their men learn about sex and romance. But you need to understand men's sexual needs.

Men do want more from sex than sex! They want *complete* relationships. Complete—meaning intimate—sexually, emotionally, spiritually, and relationally. Men do hunger for intimacy, despite the fact that many substitute sex for sharing and emotion. Some, however, are able to connect with both.

Men who tend to confuse emotional needs for sexual needs and view intimacy as sex become frustrated, grumpy, and upset when they don't have a sexual outlet. Sex is usually their only source of closeness.

Although men want sex, they are often unsure of what they really want and how to obtain it. The problem is not insurmountable. Both husband and wife need to talk, listen, and discuss their sexual needs. Many men feel more comfortable discussing sex in the darkness of the bedroom because the risk of intimate sharing is diminished there.

Dr. Archibald Hart conducted a national survey with men and the subject of male sexuality. Approximately 150 men who participated in the Hart report were asked the question, "Do you feel that women understand men's sex drive?" The "no" response was a strong 83 percent, which probably indicated a lack of sufficient sex in a relationship.[2]

What do men want their wives to understand about their sexuality? That they are normal when it comes to sex. That an understanding of one another's needs must be recognized, and that both partners must work toward mutual satisfaction.

Men want their wives to understand and accept the strength of their biological drives. The male sex drive is not a fault nor is it a mistake. God is the author of sex. Men want their wives to know that looking at other women does not mean they don't love their wives. A look of admiration is not a sign of straying.

Men want their wives to initiate lovemaking—at least part of the time. They get weary of being the pursuer, and they do appreciate some novelty.

At times men do not want sex, but they do want closeness. Often wives interpret every physical overture as a prelude to ending up in bed—sometimes for good reason. No one is a mind reader. It simplifies everything when the man verbalizes his intent and desire.[3]

As you reach out to encourage your husband with sex and romance there can be two side benefits. He will learn more, and you will be more satisfied.

There is also a relationship between sex and your language style. The visual person takes his tendency into the bedroom as well as every other room. The visual person (and remember that most men tend to be highly visual) is aroused by what he sees, and he appreciates visual detail. The decor of the bedroom as well as what a spouse wears (or doesn't wear) is part of the process of creating romance. All visual people are not responsive to the same sights. It is important for the visual spouse to share with his mate the kinds of visual stimuli he appreciates. If you have a visual spouse, ask him what sights are pleasing to him and allow time for him to look at you.

Attention to visual details is important at all stages of a romantic evening that leads to sexual expression. A restaurant that captures a romantic atmosphere with lighting, warm colors, comfortable furniture is part of the foreplay that leads to a fulfilling sexual encounter.

An auditory person may take for granted all your efforts to look good, but he will enjoy romantic music on the stereo. This is usually the time for soft, soothing music rather than a Sousa march! And don't forget to disengage the telephone, fax, beeper, and other distractions when it's time for lovemaking. The auditory partner is especially distracted by annoying sounds and interruptions.

Also, verbal expressions may be more important to this person, even during lovemaking. But be sure your auditory partner wants your verbal expressions at this time. The bottom line of romance is always doing those things that your spouse wants and avoiding those things your spouse dislikes.

A feelings-oriented man will respond best to the feel of various fabrics, the touch of the skin, and fragrances such as perfume and massage oils. Whereas a visual person may respond to the subdued atmosphere of dim candlelight, the feelings person likes the fragrance of the candle. Room temperature is also very important to the feelings-oriented individual.

Did you ever think of quietness being an enhancement to the romance or sexual life of your marriage? Most men greatly appreciate times of being quiet together especially if you're the talkative one, and he's the quiet person. A woman might be surprised by the answer when she asks her husband the question, "How much do you value your quiet time or our quiet time together?" Usually the answer indicates it's very much valued. So, what can you do? You could practice being quiet with your husband. If he tends to be quiet, give him some quiet time. Perhaps he's relaxing in a room reading or watching TV. You could go in and sit next to him without saying anything. You could read or watch TV with him.

You could invite him for a walk around the block and enforce a gag rule on yourself. Don't bring up anything unless he does and then only talk about his topics.

We all enjoy most forms of stimulation to some degree, but each of us finds some things more romantic than others. What does your husband prefer? What do you prefer? Have you really identified your specific sexual needs in this way and shared them with your spouse? Have you asked him about specific preferences? If not, why not do it soon? You may be pleased and delighted with the information you receive![4]

So this is a chapter filled with suggestions.

Saying "I love you" is a message that needs to be conveyed to your spouse every day. But creativity helps you convey the message in many ways that show you really mean it. So here are some wild and different ways to get your message across. You may feel a little silly or embarrassed trying some of these at first. But the response is well worth the effort; some of these could really connect with your husband.

Thirty Ways to Hold On to Romance

1. Find books on other languages in the library or a bookstore and copy "I love you" in several languages. Either write out the message or learn how to pronounce the message properly.

2. Write the words "I love you" backward and place the message in your husband's shoe.

3. When you steam up the bathroom, write "I love you" on the mirror and ask him to come in while it's still readable. (You might also consider taking a shower together!)

4. Put a balloon in the car with the words "I love you" on it or in it.

5. Spell "I love you" with candies on your husband's pillow, desk, or favorite chair.

6. Make a huge "I love you" banner and tape it to the ceiling over your bed.

7. Carve "I love you" in wood and float your message in the fish tank, orange juice container, or even the toilet!

8. Paint "I love you" on a household object (refrigerator, mirror, garage door, etc.) with removable paint.

9. Buy an inexpensive glider and soar it toward your husband pulling a tiny "I love you" banner (or paint "I love you" on the wings).

10. Take him kite flying. Make sure your kite says "I love you" in some creative way. (The new kites are great! My wife and I have tried this.)

11. Bake the message on or inside a pastry (cake, fortune cookie, etc.). Or put a written "I love you" message inside the Thanksgiving or Christmas turkey. Imagine your husband's reaction as he unfolds the message in front of your guests!

12. If you have a talking bird (parrot, mynah, cockatiel), see if the bird can be taught to say "I love you," adding your husband's name. (Be sure the bird doesn't have an obscene vocabulary as well!)

13. For a special occasion, write "I love you" on your eyelids so the message shows when you close your eyes.

14. If you have a telephone answering recorder leave an "I love you" message on it for him.

15. Bury or hide the message and give him a treasure map to find it. It is also nice to have a small gift with the message when the searching entails some time and effort.

16. Say "I love you" in sign language. Simply raise your right hand palm forward, lifting thumb, index finger and pinkie while keeping the two middle fingers folded down.

17. If you have a swimming pool, write "I love you" on the bottom of the pool with different objects.

18. Write "I love you" on the kitchen counter with sugar or flour.

19. If your husband keeps a daily calendar, write "I love you" messages on several of the dates.

20. Write "I love you" very small and fasten it inside his glasses or sunglasses with clear tape.

21. Tie the message to one of your pets in such a way that your husband will have to take it off the pet to read it.

22. Record "I love you" messages on videocassette or audio tape and mail it to your husband. Write a wild title on the tape's label. Be sure to put "personal" on the envelope if sending to an office.

23. Give your husband an "I love you" ornament for Christmas.

24. Purchase a dozen Valentine's cards in February and send one to your husband each month of the year.

25. Buy a package of candy and open it carefully at one of the seams. Put several love messages inside with your husband's name on them, then reseal the package. Make sure he's the one to open the candy—not the kids!

26. Purchase a book of blank pages at a stationary store. Write a love message inside using one word per page. (Be creative. The book may contain 50–100 pages.) Take the book to your public library, tell the librarian your plan and ask him/her to keep the book for you until your husband comes to claim it. Send him a card (perhaps a reserve book card purchased from the library) with a message that the library is holding a special reserved book for him.

27. Get ideas for handmade love-message cards from stationery or card stores. Be creative with size, color, and design.

28. Place an "I love you" message in the "personals" column of the local newspaper. Send him an anonymous message

to read the personals every day that week until the message is discovered.

29. Write each word from the message "I love you" on three separate sheets of paper and put each in an envelope. Ask three different friends to drop off one envelope to your husband during the week.

30. Now you can be creative. List four other ways to say "I love you" that might be special for the man in your life.[5]

Do men need to hear the words, "I love you" in order to feel loved? Yes, but more than that he needs to hear that his wife appreciates him and what he does. He wants to know that his hard work and attention to detail around the house is highly valued. Someone has said that when your relationship with your man is full of gratitude and not just actions, you'll receive feelings. Gratitude also enhances the romance and sexual relationship.

One of the ways to romance the man in your life is through food. That's right—good old basic food. The average husband finds that it's romantic when his wife makes a special meal for him. For some, mealtime is a time to connect. Going out to dinner at a nice quiet restaurant is a wonderful setting for romance. Find out what foods are really special for the man in your life. Then be creative!

When your husband is in a relaxed mood or when the two of you are out to dinner, say, "I need ten minutes of your time to conduct an interview with you. I can't tell you what it is for at this time, but you will eventually know more about it." Then ask him the following questions:

1. When you used to date in high school or college, what were your favorite types of dates? Why?

2. During those years, did you dream about an outstanding

date that you always wanted to have but never did? (I don't mean with a certain movie star!)

3. What are your favorite colors?

4. What is your favorite type of music?

5. What are your favorite travel spots to visit?

6. What are your favorite foods?

7. What type of restaurant do you like best?

8. What are your three favorite desserts?

9. What are your favorite flowers?

10. What is your favorite cologne/perfume?

11. What are your favorite types of books?

12. What shows or plays do you enjoy the most and why?

13. What three types of activities would you like to try, given a chance to do so?

The results of the interview should give you ample ideas for numerous dates, either simple or extravagant, that incorporate many of your partner's favorites.

Sexual touching is a vital part of a husband-wife relationship. But as with other forms of marital communication, touching takes time and effort to develop. The intense drive for physical contact that precedes the wedding, and lasts for a while afterward, often becomes a rut: "Well, it's Thursday night. I guess it's time to have sex again."

Each of you will differ in your desire for the expression of physical love. One of you may enjoy a great amount of bodily contact while the other is satisfied with much less. Your specific tastes for touching may also be different. One may enjoy passionate embraces, caresses, and massages while the other prefers more relaxed contact such as resting his head on his partner's lap. One may like holding hands for an hour, the other for two minutes.

In order to increase the enjoyment of physical touching in your marriage, evaluate your present experience with touching. After each of you have completed the following statements, share your responses:

- Some of the ways I like to be touched are . . .

- Some of the ways I do not like to be touched are . . .

- I think you like to be touched by . . .

- The times I like to be touched are . . .

- The times I prefer not to be touched are . . .

- I think we touch each other _____ times each day.

- Who does the most touching in our relationship?

- Who prefers to do the touching in our relationship?

- When I am touched it makes me feel . . .

- When you are touched you feel . . .

- The way we could improve our touching would be to . . . [6]

Cliff and Joyce Penner have developed the following discussion tool for couples so they can increase their understanding and enjoyment of their sexual relationship.

Common Differences to Be Negotiated

Check the ones that pertain to you on a separate piece of paper. Ask your husband to do the same.

I like to initiate._____

I like making love in the morning._____

Direct initiation is the most positive for me._____

I like to have sex several times per week._____

Regarding kisses, I like them long _____and wet _____.

I like to do a lot of talking:

    Before making love. _____

    During making love. _____

    After making love. _____

I like noisy lovemaking. _____

Explicit sexual talk is arousing for me. _____

I like to talk about it afterward. _____

I like to get _____and give _____lots of touching.

Direct stimulation is most positive for me. _____

I like to make love with the lights on. _____

I like my partner to have eyes open when lovemaking.

_____

I like oral sex when it is the woman stimulating the man.

_____

I like oral sex when it is the man stimulating the woman.

_____

I like our lovemaking experiences to be different every time. _____

I look forward to a lot of excitement and creativity. _____

For me there is a strong connection between my sexuality and my spirituality. _____

I like my spouse to initiate. _____

I like making love at night. _____

I like subtle initiation. _____

Having sex once every week or two is fine for me. _____

I like kisses to be short _____ and dry _____.

I have little need for talking:

Before making love. _____

During making love. _____

After making love. _____

I like quiet sex. _____

I like subtle and indirect sexual talk. _____

I have no need to talk about it later. _____

I don't have much need to give _____ or get _____ much touching.

I like very indirect stimulation. _____

I like the lights off. _____

I am uncomfortable being watched by my spouse in love-making. _____

I don't like oral sex when it is the woman stimulating the man. _____

I don't like oral sex when it is the man stimulating the woman. _____

I like our lovemaking experiences to be pretty much the same every time. _____

I like predictability. _____

I am not aware of much connection between my sexuality and my spirituality. _____

Each of you note any of your unique differences that need to be discussed and negotiated.[7]

Guidelines for Romantic Getaways

Here are several practical tips for those special occasions when you would like to get him alone and away from the house for a few hours or a few days.

1. *Plan Ahead Together.* When planning a getaway, write ahead to the local chamber of commerce, hotels, or resorts for brochures. Obtain information on your destination from a travel agent or your automobile club. Look over the brochures together and fantasize about your getaway, even if you will only be gone for one night. Plan your itinerary and schedule together. The planning, dreaming, and anticipating will boost your enjoyment of the event. If the getaway is a surprise for your husband, the anticipation is yours, but the enjoyment will be mutually shared.

2. *Use Discount Books.* One way to save money on getaways is to use discount books. For example, I order an

Entertainment book for the Orange County area of
Southern California. Since Joyce and I enjoy eating out
on many of our dates, the Entertainment book is a real
money saver. The book contains coupons offering two
meals for the price of one at seventy-five to one hundred
different restaurants. It was through the Entertainment
book that we discovered a very romantic restaurant located
only three miles from our home. We frequented that
restaurant for several years. There are also coupons for 50
percent discounts at many hotels. This is just one of
many discount plans.

One word of warning however: Don't scrimp too
much on a romantic getaway. You are investing in your
marriage!

3. *Communicate Your Preferences.* If your getaway will take
   you to a resort, hotel, or motel that is new to you, be sure
   to let the staff know of your special needs and wants,
   likes, and dislikes. Do you want a room with a view, a
   quiet room, or a nonsmoking room? Would you enjoy a
   fireplace, jacuzzi, or hot tub? Do you prefer a king-size
   bed, a waterbed, or twin beds? Attention to these details
   will make your getaway even more special.

4. *Cover Details at Home.* Think through and plan for all the
   details of baby-sitting, pet care, and mail and newspaper
   pickup before you leave so you don't need to think abut
   them while you are gone. Make a list of what needs to be
   done beforehand as well as important tasks that will need
   your attention when you return. Some couples even use a
   preplanned getaway checklist. If one of you is Mr. or
   Mrs. Super-checker-upper, write yourself a note assuring
   that you have checked up on everything at least twice!

Now that our children are out of the home, Joyce and

I no longer need a babysitter when we get away. But we do need a combination housesitter and petsitter to care for two golden retrievers, two hundred tropical fish, and the yard.

5. *Establish Ground Rules.* There are some things that should be excluded from a romantic getaway. A list of mutually agreed upon ground rules may help set the stage for the romantic atmosphere you're getting away for. No talking about work or the children. No talking about conflicts, in-laws, bills, or other irritating topics. Don't worry about staying on diets. Do not take briefcases or make phone calls to the office. Take along recreational reading only. Make a commitment to unplug the TV while you are there. Yes, you heard me correctly. Unplug the television even if major sports events are on!

6. *Don't Overplan.* Allow gaps in your getaway schedule to relax and loaf and talk and love. Practice spontaneity.

7. *Emergencies Only.* If you are going away for several days, tell your friends and relatives that you don't want to hear from them unless an emergency arises. And be sure to define what you mean by an emergency.

8. *Spread the Word.* Tell everyone you meet on your outing—hotel clerks, waiters, bellhops—that this is one of your romantic getaways. You'll be surprised how many people will do their best to help you enjoy your special event.

9. *Pray Together.* Set aside special times for prayer, perhaps focusing your prayer on thankfulness for your sexual relationship as suggested in chapter 9. Read portions of the Song of Solomon aloud to each other for your devotions.

10. *Share Love Words.* Tell each other how much you love one another using many thoughtful and creative approaches. Share your romantic memories together—a favorite getaway in the past, a memorable card or letter, an outstanding lovemaking interlude you recall. Also plan what you are going to share with friends and family when they ask you where you went on your getaway and what you did. Again, be creative![8]

One of the best steps that you can take for your husband, yourself, and for your marriage is to become experts about the sexual relationship. Even today in our sexually-oriented society most men and women are still quite uninformed about the sexual process. Ask the typical man if he's ever read a book on sex and his answer is, "I don't need to read any book. I know all about it. I'm a great lover!" That's a myth! Perhaps in his dreams.

That's why one of the best steps you can take to encourage your husband is to go out, purchase the following books, and suggest you read the first one mentioned out loud to one another.

The Celebration of Sex by Doug Rosenau would be my recommendation. The book *52 Ways to Have Fun, Fantastic Sex* by Cliff and Joyce Penner would give you some creative ideas, and then a book that you might want to give your husband as a gift is *Men and Sex* by Cliff and Joyce Penner.

By the time you finish these resources you will be knowledgeable. You never know where you will find practical enlightening information. Now, consider these suggestions.

1. *Laugh*

God had quite a sense of humor when He designed sex. Think of getting your bodies together and doing what you do in a sexual experience. When you sit back and think about the uniqueness of the sex act, it's actually hilarious. And to think of the incredibly great feelings that happen in your bodies by doing such rollicking acts is awesome.

2. *Experiment*
To experiment is to test or try how something works or discover something new. You cannot fail when you experiment because there is no predetermined outcome.

3. *Surprise*
If surprises are not negative for the other spouse, a little surprising action or gesture can clearly send the message of thoughtfulness. For the spouse who prefers predictability, plan your surprises together. Sexual surprises will add a lot of fun for the two of you.

4. *Shock*
A little shock, a slight shake-up, or a new burst of interest, excitement, or adrenaline is a source of energy to get you connected with each other and bring passion.

5. *Treat*
Treats are endless resources of sexual fun. Treats can fall into these main categories: purchases, accouterments, preparation, attention, and activities.

6. *Pleasure*
You can never go wrong if you focus on pleasure. If both of you are taking responsibility for doing what feels good to you and respecting what feels good to the other, the giving and receiving of pleasure is guaranteed not to fail. Pleasure or pleasing refers to skin-to-skin touch that has no demand for arousal or orgasm or any response or action. It is just for the sake of touching and being touched. No demand means exactly that. There is no

expectation; your and his responses to the touch can be pleasant, warm, comfortable, enjoyable, arousing, or neutral. The pleasuring can be an end in itself, or it can lead to an erotic lovemaking experience.

The woman best serves the man by allowing herself to be aware of her sexuality and to share it openly with him. Remember, nothing turns a man on more than a turned-on woman. And as you are able to discover and know yourself and share yourself freely and openly with him, he will feel served.

Sex is about the process of enjoying pleasure, not about your pleasing him or his pleasing you. Mutual pleasure is the refrain of sexual fulfillment. Ultimately, your husband will be pleased only when you are pleased, and you will be pleased only when you respond to your natural instincts of extending and enjoying pleasure. When you listen to and pursue your need for pleasure, you will be totally satisfied. Then he, too, will be satisfied. Hence, you serve him most by pursuing your sexuality and making sure you are pleased.

Sexual expertise is learned. We hope the two of you can become authorities on yourselves and communicate your awareness of your likes and dislikes to each other. You can become sex experts with each other. Your husband can't know your sexual hungers unless you tell him. Since you are likely to change in your preferences from one time to another, telling him once is not enough.[9]

Chapter
7

*Encouragement is one of the finest
expressions of love.*

Chapter 7

~

How Women Are
Encouraging Men—The
Women Speak Out

It's encouraging to see how many women, and wives in particular, are involved in the process of encouraging the men in their lives. The accounts in this chapter come directly from women who responded to our survey. They are honest and direct. As you read them you may wonder, "Would I be willing to do that?" You may discover some new ways to respond or end up feeling like you're doing a pretty good job already.

Listen to their stories . . .

"I encourage my husband by being attentive to his words, actions, and desires. I know that he wants to honor the Lord, cherish me, and protect me. (Sometimes I choose to believe this.)"

~

"Finances is a key area where I have to work the most. The strings of the purse seem to be the strings to his heart. Watching expenditures and keeping good records are key."

"Discipline of our children has been a struggle. Inspiring them to be attentive, obedient, and respectful involves my attitudes, prayer life, and acts of love (including punishment for wrongdoing/attitudes).

"Being content and showing gratefulness is encouraging to him. Finding little expressions (favorite foods, etc.) of love to serve him keeps our intimate life in good repair."

"We encourage each other, but I haven't ever really thought about how. I am always there for him and whatever endeavor he is into, be it craft work, yard and garden, travel, children. He is retired and wants the companionship of an at-home wife, but also allows me to pursue my interests and career both in the workplace and at home. In return, I try to accommodate him with a schedule that allows me to continue working but gives us maximum time together for our leisure time pursuits."

"I try to always ask about his day and if something has been amiss or troubling, perhaps give suggestions how it might be improved or helped or encourage him to do. I always make a point to ask the night before what is on his agenda for the next day or even next week and encourage him to 'hang in there' or 'have a great day.' Also I always tell him I love him several times during the day—like before he leaves and when the day is over.

"I also try to let him know how much I appreciate it

when he does things for me or generally keeps the house, yard, and cars in tiptop shape."

"My father was an alcoholic that we all 'practiced' diligently to keep happy—at all costs. It was hard work and I now struggle against this aspect! It's a hard balance.

"My husband is an artist who I encouraged to quit his 9–5 steady job in order to use the gifts that God has given him. That was almost 4 years ago—financially it has been a struggle, but spiritually we have both grown by leaps and bounds in learning to trust the Lord.

"I pray over him when he is asleep (probably 6 years ago he was not walking with the Lord). I used Colossians 1:9–14 (all the women in my prayer group have used this with miraculous results!). 'For this reason, since the day we heard about you, we have not stopped praying for you and asking God to fill you with the knowledge of His will through all spiritual wisdom and understanding. And we pray this in order that you may live a life worthy of the Lord and may please Him in every way: bearing fruit in every good work, growing in the knowledge of God, being strengthened with all power according to His glorious might so that you may have great endurance and patience, and joyfully giving thanks to the Father, who has qualified you to share in the inheritance of the saints in the kingdom of light. For He has rescued us from the dominion of darkness and brought us into the kingdom of the Son He loves, in whom we have redemption, the forgiveness of sins.'

"I encourage my husband by using reflecting listening on spiritual issues and acknowledging that he approaches Christianity from a different angle than I do. I encourage him by verbalizing his strengths that I love as a parent, husband, and artist."

—⁓—

"As a woman I was taught to support my husband in any way possible, and he would return the favor. I watched my mother for years soothe my father and continue to encourage him to follow his dreams. Sometimes that seems so hard to do.

"Society likes us to believe that we need to look out for #1. As women, we should not allow any man to have dominion over us. This worldly view does not fit the teaching of our Lord. The decision to do what was right and not what was best is still a rather conscious thing.

"What I did find when I made the decision to support my husband was a great joy. Now, when he tells me his dreams, I don't wonder what is going to happen to me. I try to be his sounding board. A spring for him to bounce new things off of. If I remained rigid and worried I could never help him obtain his dreams. The wonderful thing about it is that all I had to do is hang on and ride the ride.

"I'm not saying that everything has turned out the way it was dreamed up. But it has been an adventure that I would never want to replace. My support has allowed both him and me to venture out, to follow the dreams that the Lord has given us.

"Simple things like listening about his day, his dreams, and his hopes. Praying with him and for him. Hearing out his ideas for our future without wondering what is in it for me. These are things that I try to do to support my husband."

—⁓—

"I pray for and with him. I began working to help alleviate some of his responsibilities and time spent earning money. We have more time together now.

"It is an encouragement to him when I go with him to the job site on the weekends to finish up a job.

"I encourage my father frequently. I send him random letters (not a Christmas or birthday letter) and reminisce of times when I was a child and the things he did that impacted my life, or thanking him for wisdom imparted to me and how it has helped me when it came time for me to raise my children. I call often.

"He was encouraged when I urged him to share his navy days with my son. It caused him to open up and share his grief of lost comrades with his family. He also brought up triumphant times."

⌒

"When my husband and I first met, he talked about going on an out-of-state hunt with his father before his dad couldn't go anymore. Last year the opportunity came for him and his dad to go hunting (elk) in the Colorado Rockies. I encouraged my husband to go and tried to help him find ways of financing his trip.

"When they got back my husband was just like a little boy in a candy store. He had been able to fulfill a longtime dream and bag a huge six-point bull elk, the head of which I'll be living with for years to come, as he wanted to get it mounted.

"In turn, he brags about how great his wife is to all the guys he works with and encourages me in other things that I do. He also tells me constantly how grateful to God he is that we are married."

"First off, a person knows how their spouse really feels. Honest, pure love and acceptance shines through a quiet spirit and loving demeanor. I make it a point to see the best in my spouse, and encourage, encourage, encourage. We enjoy a very close and loving marriage in part because of this. I am also very thankful for my spouse and I very regularly let him know. In other words, he knows he's appreciated."

"By acknowledging and praising him for the accomplishments he has made. Suggesting new ideas or skills to pursue and committing to trying them with my spouse. When faced with a decision, helping him see the various options he can take and supporting his decisions.

"Helping him see the positive sides to situations without accusing him of being negative or pessimistic."

"My husband and I have been married for close to seven years. My role as an encourager is one that I am always working on. There were a few years when my husband was really struggling with what he wanted to do with his life. This was a question I had in my own life, but it was a greater barrier for him. I encouraged him then by being supportive of ideas he had as he thought through options. I gave him a gift of a gym membership which he had not had for a year or two . . . because I know that in his life, the physical discipline sets the pace for other areas of his life.

"Since this time, he has pursued a graduate program and is just a few months from completion. My support has been financial and emotional as he has taken on a difficult academic/internship schedule. His grades are excellent and he has been graciously guided to a field where his gifts are wonderfully evident. I remind him of this and of his journey so that he can be encouraged by his growth as a person on many levels. While at times I play the martyr, I have also grown. I try to see beyond the immediate sacrifices and am then able to celebrate his sense of direction and purpose and our growth as a couple laying the foundation for our future.

"Other ways I have tried to encourage my husband are less verbal and more practical. I am slowly learning to choose his 'side' when we are faced with responsibilities through church, family, school, etc. and he makes a choice not to participate. In short, I don't try to make him go places and do things unless it is what he wants. We are very independent with independent interests and activities, so when there are shared areas, it is difficult to bite my tongue . . . but as I do, it has been an encouragement to him—knowing that I am supporting his choice for how he uses his time. He does the same for me, and it has been very positive."

"To encourage my husband, I try to treat him as I would wish to be treated. Recently my husband had an interview, and I knew that he was putting a lot of pressure on himself to get the job. But to me, he is more important. I told him that I love him and that some silly job was not going to make that big a difference in our lives. He may not have gotten that job, but I feel that it was so very important for him to hear those words, that I am not putting additional pressure on him. That I believe in his talents, work ethic, and sweet spirit. That I know him well enough to say that truly if they did not hire him, that was their loss.

"I also try to encourage him by encouraging his interests and activities. Like allowing him space for his Men's Meeting once a week. Sometimes I have to say that when I come home tired, this is really the last thing I look forward to in my home, but I know that it is important to him so I try to allow him the time and space for his meetings.

"I also pray for him. When we pray together, I pray that the Lord will help him in areas that he has shared with me. I pray for things that he is concerned about."

───────

"I encourage my husband by supporting him in all that he does. I let him know that I am praying for him. I thank him for the things he does for me when he goes out of his way to do it. I lift him up in the presence of others and let them know how wonderful and how kind he is.

"I have on occasion let him know how smart (intelligent) that I think he is. I've even made the comment to others that for a person who has never had any professional training, i.e., college, etc., he is very knowledgeable about the Bible. He's just very wise and smart.

"He is a very kind, smart, gentle, loving husband and father, and has a lot of patience. And I express this to him verbally periodically. When I tell him verbally or in actions how I feel about him, I can see his face light up and the tension release."

───────

"I have such a loving and sensitive husband. I try to always be aware of when he does things for me. I will compliment and thank him for fixing dinner, taking out the trash, changing the bottled water, keeping his desk straight, and making the bed.

"But most of all I let him know how much it means to me that we spend time in God's Word and prayer together. I love him so. He's the best. I respect and admire him."

~⌇⌇~

"My husband and I have known each other since September of 1985. We were friends and never anything else till three years ago. Oddly enough today is our second wedding anniversary. We never dreamed in a million years we'd marry each other. We're still in awe of that fact. We know each other backward and forward. He was and still is my best friend through our adolescent years, my first marriage, my first child's death, and my second child's birth, and now he is his 'Daddy.' He was there for all of it. And vice versa. I know his dreams and goals and support him in everything he does, unless I feel like it will be harmful to him physically, emotionally, or spiritually, or to us. I encourage him. He is very hard on himself. He sets his expectations very high, but it keeps him successful at work. He's in construction and uses his high standards to be a good leader. He is an excellent husband and father, but he doesn't see himself that way. We know and understand our faults as well. We see each other's strengths and weaknesses. We never argue; we just have discussions. I could go on and on.

"My dad and I have a very similar relationship. I was brought up in an open-minded, open-hearted home. I never saw my parents fight. They would have discussions and weren't afraid to have them in front of my sister and me; and at times they even included us. My parents have been married twenty-eight years this May. I pray our marriage is similar to theirs. I love my husband like my mom loves hers. She taught us how to be a good wife like she is. She's a beautiful woman, and I pray we can learn from her as we already have."

⌒

"I don't encourage my husband like I should. My experience is that men like to be encouraged by making them feel important. They also like to feel appreciated. The more you tell them they are appreciated, the better they feel about themselves. Men usually don't feel appreciated. They work a job all day and come home, and it goes on day after day. Humdrum life. When you tell them how important they are in your life, they try harder to please you and hold their head up a little higher. Damaging words cause the opposite effect. When he comes home, he needs to be told he was missed and that I am glad he is home. I want him to know he's important."

⌒

"My form of encouragement to my husband has been to let him know that he was created in Christ's image and whether or not he believes it, God has forgiven him and does see him as a new creation; old things are passed away.

"I also let him know that God has given him power and talents and that as he steps out on faith, God will give him the desires of his heart. Believing and receiving!

"My father died a horrible death, and I guess the best encouragement I gave my dad is that when everyone else was afraid to hug and kiss him, I kissed him and hugged him and let him know no matter what happened, I would never stop loving him! Never."

⌒⌒⌒

"I make my husband meals, tell him how much I appreciate him, buy him things he needs/wants, and make him special gifts. I write him notes, call him during the day to tell him how much I appreciate him, and I listen to him. I am his biggest fan!"

⌒⌒⌒

"One of the ways that I encourage my husband is by speaking positively about him in public and especially in front of my two daughters. At a job which I had in the past, I was actually criticized by a group of coworkers because I never complained about my husband. They did not appreciate me not taking part in their miserable men stories. While my husband is not perfect, I have no desire to tear him down in front of others. I have often told my girls to look for husbands just like their daddy. Sometimes he hears these compliments and sometimes he doesn't, but I know he is well aware of his girls' love and respect for him. They truly do feel that Daddy 'hung the moon.' I sincerely feel that he is one of the best fathers I have ever known and I work to make him aware of that. I try to let him know when he does special things my father did not do for me and how meaningful those actions are to girls.

"The times that it is most difficult to encourage my husband is when he is feeling depressed and angry with himself. It is during these times I try to keep the home environment quiet, ask little or nothing from him, and listen intently when he does share his feelings. Sometimes he doesn't talk, and I know he needs me to confirm that he is in control, that he is a great man, and that I desire to pursue him in the physical relationship. Actually I know that the latter is probably my best encourager of all for him during these times.

"I forget often that he is encouraged by my telling him how handsome he is, and sometimes I just let him know how glad I am that I married him. When I see other men at church and how they respond to their wives, I tell him how glad I am I didn't marry any of them.

"My sister's mother-in-law made a very negative statement about my husband's weight once during a family gathering. While I've been raised to keep angry feelings inside . . . I let my displeasure out with this woman, and she became quite upset. She left the gathering in a huff, and I was mortified at what I had done. My husband's feelings were not hurt by her statement, but I think he was surprised and pleased when he heard about my quick defense.

"I know I can never outdo my husband in this area. He is the master of encouragement and has helped me and my self-esteem tremendously. This writing has made me aware of my need to do more.

"In the past I don't believe I have been much of an encourager of my father. Now that he is eighty-three and our relationship has softened, I find that helping him relive some of the wonderful vacations we took in the past seems to encourage him. He loves to talk about past events, especially things that we did as a family. He often becomes depressed when he stops and thinks of what little time he and my mom have left together. I try to encourage him to rather focus on the almost sixty years they have shared and how blessed they have been to have this time."

"I mention the strength of my husband in his presence when I lead a Family Enrichment Seminar for our congregation. I write down his strengths or my appreciation to him as many ways as his age on his birthday cards every year.

"When I am proud of my children, I say to them where my husband can hear, 'You look like your dad on that point! I am proud of you!'"

⌒

"My way of encouraging my husband is to wake up at 6:30 each morning to cook him a hearty breakfast. He feels very much cared for and loved (so he says). I also verbally express my affections for him. I also help him with his church responsibilities. Since I have a background in banking, he feels that I can be of great help to him, so I do try to help.

"I didn't have a very close relationship with my dad. He didn't show much emotion and was mostly quiet (except on moral issues). I don't recall doing much to encourage my dad."

⌒

"I try to encourage my husband by praying for him. I encourage my husband by listening to him and giving him feedback on his ideas and projects.

"I encourage him by telling him where I see him doing a good job. Be it with the kids, in his farmwork, at church or in his personal growth (or even putting up with me)."

⌒

"I try to thank him for all the good, kind things he does. I try to not take his creativity for granted nor his efforts to help me however he can.

"I respect him, his spiritual leadership, his integrity, his perseverance. I block off time for us to spend together, alone, to revitalize and recharge."

⁓

"I encourage my husband by supporting/joining him in church activities. I listen to his ideas, concerns, and such. I help him brainstorm plans for his churchwork. I hold him when he comes home from work and especially after a hard day. I prepare meals he enjoys. I plan dates with him, especially on the two mornings a week when I don't work and he can go into work later.

"He is not particularly spontaneous and likes me to plan unexpected outings or dates. He loves Snickers candy bars and I buy these for him sometimes. I rub his shoulders and sometimes his feet. When he comes home I encourage the children to welcome him enthusiastically so he has a big welcome from us all. I also verbally tell him I love and need him especially when we are intimate.

"Sometimes I feel I encourage him by not telling him about mundane, irritating things and just handle them myself and not overburden him with such things."

⁓

"I spend lots of time with him and try to schedule activities he will enjoy. I ask for his advice and opinions. I pass on compliments he has received from others. Help him in his career efforts whenever I can. Keep a calm and peaceful home that is always in good order and clean. Promote happy relationships within our family (he was raised in a difficult and contentious environment) and lots of family celebrations together. Remember to remind him of things that he forgets (appointments, etc. He is not highly organized by nature!).”

⌒

“I try hard to be a sounding board for him about his job and feelings about his coworkers. I tell him what a great father he is and tell him that the time he spends with his children is important because they need a father’s input and outlook on life.

“For my father in his last years of his life, I encouraged him with my love and that of his grandchildren because his will to live was very low. I can say our love always brought a smile to his face.”

⌒

“I listen carefully, and I do less talking. I support him in his interests. It’s easy because they are also mine. I tell him often that I love him and appreciate him. I show respect for him because I honestly feel it.”

⌒

“There are many ways in which I hope I encourage my husband. We’ve been married for 30 years, and during that time I’ve learned so much and I know I will learn a lot more.

“First, I always try to compliment my husband daily. I find specific things to affirm him in. As a pastor’s wife I encourage him by supporting his ministry. Not just verbally, but by being involved . . . using my gifts and abilities to enhance his ministry. Submissively supporting him whether I necessarily always agree with him or not. I say good things about my husband in front of others and then let him know I did.

"I also try to keep him sexually satisfied which I've found is a part of encouragement. I allow him to be the spiritual leader and in doing so am encouraging him in his role in our family. Do I do all of these things perfectly and consistently? No. But, with God's help I am trying to be an encourager."

———

"I write out thoughts and feelings about him in creative ways and give them to him as gifts.

"Pray for him and with him.

"Focus my attention on our kids so that he can relax. Show consistency in my parenting so that he does not have to be the 'heavy' when kids misbehave.

"I kidnap him for a getaway trip to amusement parks. We play and eat junk food all day.

"I make sure I'm fully dressed (clothes, makeup, hair) with a fresh look when he comes home at night.

"I leave messages on his work recorder to say how much I love him and miss him through the day.

"I make appointments to discuss problem issues which usually he automatically clears time for.

"I don't yell; it completely shuts him down."

———

"I have always thought it most important for my husband to always know he's the love of my life. That I believe he is #1 in my life! I pray for him and try to support him, especially when the world tries to shatter him. I try to keep the homefront running as smoothly as possible, so he doesn't have to be concerned about household stuff. I don't bother him during his naps. I let him rest in peace. (Ha!)

"I try to let him know that the family and I totally respect his opinions and input. I tell him I love him on a regular basis. Hugs, kisses, pecks!!!"

"I think the way I best encourage my husband is by making our home an oasis for him. When I try to define oasis, several ideas come to mind but the most significant is:

Open
And
Safe
In
Side

"If our home can truly be the one place that is always open and safe for my husband, I believe he will be an encouraged man. He knows he is loved, accepted, wanted, and admired just as he is, even on the less-than-best days.

"My husband's job keeps him out late many evenings. He has expressed the leap of joy in his heart when he walks in and sees the bedroom light on. He knows he will have the opportunity to talk, share, and connect before going to sleep. Where I used to think nothing about going to bed early without him, now I make it a habit to wait up for him and look forward to our time together.

"I also try to give genuine compliments to my husband at home. I brag on his fathering, his handiness, the way he has completed jobs, etc. At church I compliment activities, finesse in hard situations, and insights."

"I encourage my husband by listening to him. I have talked to our four children about giving him space when he comes home so that he has some time to unwind. That gives us time to talk about his day. I desire to know all about it; the people he's talked to, the meetings he had, what he's created today.

"I defend him and lift him up to others. I listen to him when he's discouraged and help him find the answers he is searching for. I confront him when he is wrong."

———◦———

"My husband needs a lot of encouragement. He is a touch person. Hugs and kisses and pats on the back do wonders for him.

"I need to tell him often of my love and to affirm the things that he does and says. I try to encourage him to do things that I feel are his strengths. When he helps at home or with the kids I try to tell him how much I appreciate it.

"I don't give my husband enough encouragement but those are the ways that he seems to need and those are the ways I try to contribute."

———◦———

"I encourage my husband by being there for him. I attend his ball games and other things that are important to him. I take a day off from work each week so that I can spend it with him in order to refresh him and uplift him in his life. It is important to him to spend time with me. He says that it recharges his soul's batteries and helps him to be able to effectively do the things that his work demands from him. So I carve out time each week to spend especially with him doing activities which please him. I also let him take his naps when he needs to.

"My husband is very important to me, and I value him greatly. When I can write little notes, make him special things, attend functions with him, and spend time with him just because, I know that I am pleasing him and encouraging him."

⌒

"Knowing that God has called my husband to minister in a specific geographic location, He is always my source of strength to encourage my husband. The Lord has given us a vision for our community, and we know that the vision will be accomplished. Therefore, I encourage my husband by speaking words of 'reminders' to him. 'The Lord has equipped you for this purpose. You can do it through the strength of the Lord.'

"When others have deserted him, I remain by his side. We discuss what we can learn from this experience and try to grow from it.

"On my husband's day off, we escape from our little town and spend time together. I listen to his discouragements, his dreams, and we dream together.

"I constantly pray, 'Lord, help me to be the wife my husband needs.'"

⌒

"I encourage my husband with verbal praise. Words of affirmation, gratitude. Especially when he does things for others. Also when he does things around the house (dishes, laundry, garbage)—I make sure to comment on it.

"I encourage my father in the same way. I use a lot of the 'I believe in you' statements before he takes on something new. Recently my father was helping to edit Spanish home-group material. I thanked him for his work and told him he did great work."

⸻

"I encourage my husband by praising him when he does something special which I have not asked him to do. Thanking him when I have asked for his help, and he goes out of his way to help. Encouraged him to reach out to others who have hurt him in the family. Let his family know when he has done a good deed so he knows I appreciate him.

"For a while I prayed for my father to have a close walk with God. I claimed the verse where God turns the king's heart. I told my father I loved him and called him on the phone weekly to find out what was going on with him."

⸻

"This is a humbling experience for me because I don't feel I am encouraging my husband enough. I probably encourage others more than him.

"In reality I try to support him by praying for him on a daily basis. I also try to support him in ministry by using hospitality with people he is ministering to.

"I try to listen to him share dreams or frustrations and be a sounding board for him.

"I try to make our home a cheerful, pleasant place to come home to as a security from the stresses of life out there."

⸻

"My husband knows I am behind him all the way. When he lost his job (after thirteen years at a big company), he knew I didn't mind when he started his own company. We took on the new challenge. I offered to go to work if he wanted or needed me to. We cut all corners possible—I buy store brands, read books from the library, make gifts, clip coupons, plus not shop at the mall too often. I praise his work in front of the children. I do everything possible to make him know he is important—notes on the computer, hugs and kisses, never cut him down in front of anyone else, enjoy being with him, go out on dates, send him cards, tell him that I appreciate specific aspects of his personality. I also reassure him that procrastinating with the ironing is not a reflection of how much I think about him.

"It is different that he is the one who likes to sit down and talk every night. (Isn't it usually the other way around?) But I try to remember, so he doesn't have to remind me because it is so important to him. I also pray for him, the most important thing."

"I encourage my husband with verbal praise. I laughingly tell him he is the best husband I have ever had. I tell him he looks good when he dresses up for a date with me, and I always remember to thank him when we do something special, like going out to dinner or a movie.

"My father has been ill for several years. I have attempted to encourage him, because words just don't suffice for his serious medical situation, by sending him cards, cartoons, jokes, and other humorous things in the mail. This helps when I can't be there in person to comfort him."

"It seems strange to answer how I encourage my husband and father when, from my perception, they encourage me far more than I encourage them. Their encouragement comes through verbal statements about how much they believe in me and by very concrete help they give to me. They seem to anticipate my needs and constantly help me in all aspects of my life—from the minute details to the big issues."

⁓

"Positive praise works best. I thank him over and over again for filling my car with gas or for getting the oil changed. When he's slaving in the yard I bring him lemonade without being asked—keep the glass full!

"When he helps me in the kitchen, I give him lots of hugs and pats and compliments. Works every time. Also, praise, genuine praise, in front of our friends works miracles."

⁓

"There is one area that we left out in our response to your survey of encouragement of wives to husbands. That area covers the subject of hearing loss which becomes a problem to all of us sooner or later. To my husband it was 'sooner.'

"Because our daughter became profoundly deaf from meningitis in her early years, we are well aware of the problems of the hearing impaired. But then came the situation of half-hearing and half-deaf to an energetic hearing man—my husband—who is independent, a natural born leader, and loves to sing.

"Fortunately, vanity is not a problem so wearing hearing aids is no big deal. But leading the Sunday school class and not being able to hear prayer requests became humiliating and embarrassing. Barbershop singing has been a fun-filled hobby but is becoming more frustrating because of not being able to hear enough to harmonize. We now have a special phone that can be adjusted to a high volume, but even then some callers have voices difficult to understand.

"These are a few of the obstacles we are trying to hurdle as we grow old together. My job of encouraging my husband falls into two obvious categories—physical and mental.

"The physical: Seating guests so that light shines on their faces as we visit. Expression reading is something we begin to do to understand speech. For instance, my husband takes his binoculars to stage shows—he says he 'hears' better with them!

"Entertaining small groups so that one person at a time is speaking. A hubbub of noise only causes confusion. Being available to listen or speak on the phone if he cannot understand the other party. Trying to be subtle about interpreting in a group if he has not been able to understand what is being discussed. Speaking louder.

"Try to be in the same room for communication. We have devised a signal. For instance if I need help with the computer I just 'hoo-hoo,' and hearing this he comes to me!

"The mental: Patience and understanding and a SENSE OF HUMOR. Try to solve the frustration of getting communication mixed up because of not hearing the 'whole.' Relax and let it go. For instance, if he is heading for the door to do grocery shopping, I may yell after him, 'Oh yes, get some milk too.' His mind is on putting keys into the auto ignition, he hears my voice and assumes I am saying, 'Drive safely!' Then he is on his way to the store only to return with no milk. It is easy to grumble in this situation and say, 'But I told you . . .' 'But I didn't hear you!,' would be the response.

"Know that hearing aids are not cheap and new ones

must be ordered periodically because hearing usually decreases. Be willing to put new aids on the top of the list of material needs.

"The Spiritual: Being equally yoked, according to the Scriptures, and doing things together has been our anchor. We both know that God is in charge of our lives and that He will get us through our problems. Open communication is easy at times, difficult at other times. Praying gets me through this. I am not as open as my husband and tend to harbor hurt feeings. When all is said and done, these feelings are usually not warranted.

"By the way, a SMILE and a locking of eyes of understanding get us through many difficult situations."

As you read through these stories, what was your response? What did you learn? What did you feel?

Did you notice that several told of the positive effect this had on their husbands? The biblical teaching, "Do unto others as you would have them do unto you" does work!

It is apparent that these women have discovered what encourages their husbands and in some cases their fathers. Let's summarize:

The responses involve listening, being grateful, being frugal, being available, accommodating, showing appreciation, being informed, offering suggestions, believing in his abilities, praising him, praying over him, supporting his dreams, listening to his dreams and hopes without being threatened by them, going with him to his work, sending notes and letters, praying together, encouraging him to share his past experiences with his children, looking for the best in him, acknowledging accomplishments, clarifying issues for him, helping rather than accusing, reminding him of his gifts and abilities, taking his side, believing in his ideas with him, telling him "I love you" regardless, giving him space, supporting him and telling him specifics of what is appreciated.

These women do not take their men for granted. They tell him he's missed, how God sees him, and are willing cheerleaders. They tell the children how special he is, cook his favorite breakfast, block off time together, hold him, plan dates, handle irritating things for him rather than dumping on him, ask his advice and opinions, act as a sounding board, keep him sexually satisfied, dress for him, provide an atmosphere of safety, teach their children to give Dad quiet time, touch him, and are there for him.

Peggy Campolo shares how she encourages her husband, Tony:

> In my own marriage, I learned long ago that my husband appreciates the time and effort I put into helping him with the letters and articles he writes or ideas he wants to discuss, more than he does any time I spend decorating (or even cleaning!) our house. Yet I have a good friend whose husband is simply delighted to have a beautiful setting to which to come home to each evening. She pleases him by fixing fresh flowers, frequently rearranging the furniture, and making their home a lovely place. Each of us has learned a different way of showing love for her own special person.
>
> It's easy to do what you think your spouse should appreciate. The challenge is to figure out what he or she really wants, and the fun is to learn how to provide whatever it is better than anyone else possibly could![1]

The possibilities are endless! What are you doing to encourage your man? What will you do differently in the future? Encouragement is one of the finest expressions of love.

Chapter
8

Our call to encourage is not dependent upon
the other person's response.

Chapter 8

How Women *Are* Encouraging
Men—The Men Speak Out

Women *are encouraging men.* They tend to be nurturers and relational anyway. But it was helpful to hear men report about how their wives encourage them. The responses varied. Some were very basic, others were complex. What is encouraging to one man may not be encouraging to another. You need to discover what your man needs and adapt your responses to him.

Encouragement is often a two-way street in the sense that it is easier to encourage when it is appreciated and reciprocated. I'm sure that some of these men who were interviewed were responding in such a manner that it was easy for the women in their lives to encourage them.

An example of this came from this middle-aged man. "My wife frequently affirms her love for me. She takes an interest in my interests. She may not necessarily join in, but she gives a listening ear. She usually tries to make my favorite meals.

"We talk to each other frequently—we both enjoy talking. I always call her while I'm away on business trips. We always touch base once a day during my trips. I help her in the kitchen as soon as I get home from work. I help set the table, do the dishes, etc. I ask for her input when I need to make a decision. She appreciates the fact that I value her opinion."

What woman wouldn't love to encourage a man like that! But regardless of the response of the other person, we are called to be encouragers. Our call to encourage is not dependent upon the other person's response.

A young man wrote: "My wife truly cares about me and lets me know that she cares. She listens when I talk, she supports me in everything that I do, and she is positive and joyful about life. We have fun together.

"My goal is to make my wife feel special and loved. I try to take every opportunity to tell her how much she means to me. I love to do the unexpected for her. I want to make life enjoyable for her."

The following responses came from a couple in their seventies. It was interesting to hear how a man thought his wife was encouraging him and then to hear her share how she tried to encourage him. The husband said: "During the more than fifty years of our marriage, my wife has developed some delightful patterns of behavior which encourage me.

"On occasion when I've been dressed up to go somewhere, she will say, 'My, you are handsome!' Several times she has complimented me on teaching a Sunday school lesson. Sometimes she will refer to me as 'Boss.' I take this with a grain of salt, for in the next sentence she'll ask me to take the trash out.

"Although she hasn't put a statue of me anywhere, she often does little things to demonstrate her trust, her respect, and her love for me. Just as the pilot of the airliner revs up the motor to start down the runway for the takeoff, she will slide her hand under mine. As I am about to ask the blessing at a meal, she will put her hand on the table to be covered by mine. At a special time during a movie or play, she may circle my arm with hers— all little loving contacts—all initiated by her and that's what makes these actions so special. What would I like her to do in the future? Just more of the same. Y'see, real love is an action—love so demonstrated is a true encouragement."

His wife added: "The first thing that comes to mind is that I try not to be discouraging. In our lifetime, as with most people married more than fifty years, we have had dramatic personal experiences. We found that when one was down, the other offered a balance of supportive understanding. The latter did not necessarily come in a verbal response but a hug, pat on the back, or holding hands.

"When my husband brought work problems home, I tried to listen. Our daughter made an interesting observation one time. She said that, 'Whatever Mom was doing when Dad got home she would stop, sit down, and talk (or listen).' I was unaware that this was my habit.

"I found that I have a sensitive husband. He is crushed by criticism. Being aware of this I try to hold my tongue. But being human and a talkative person, things DO slip out. With effort I many times say nothing, like when we are ready to walk out the door and the tie is totally wrong for the suit. But the times I do openly criticize, there is hurt and anger. We try to solve this by my setting out the clothes before he gets dressed. I now know that he really doesn't give a hoot what he wears as long as it is comfortable and has lots of pockets!

"I find it helpful to offer encouragement by planting positive seeds and withholding negative comments. My husband was in such a profession (medical physician) that he had heard enough tragedy and unhappy stories at the office and needed a happy atmosphere to come home to.

"It is not difficult to offer an honest comment of admiration when my husband really looks great. I guess that would be a form of encouragement.

"My husband and I purposefully did not discuss our thoughts before we each wrote our comments. It was fascinating to later read each other's paper and find similarities. Oh yes, one more thought. A sense of humor has played an important role during the tense times. My husband is better at it than I, however! There is nothing like a good laugh."

As you read these responses from the men ask yourself three questions.

1. Is this the way my man would like to be encouraged?

2. In what way am I doing this at the present time?

3. How might it affect our relationship if I responded in this way?

"The most encouragement I get from my wife comes from the fact that she has stayed with me for eighteen years. It is indicative of a commitment to the marriage above what I deserve. She is loyal and faithful, unconditionally. These things translate to me as a commitment to me that is a tremendous encouragement. She stands by me, supports me, and defends me not only when others would consider it appropriate, but when they probably would not.

"In a consistent pattern she compromises to do things I like to do. She is always willing and ready to assist with projects that bring me recognition. Often these find her doing the majority of the work with little of the credit.

"I can't think of anything else she could reasonably be expected to do to encourage me more."

Here is a man who appreciates loyalty, support, recognition, and adaptability. In what way do you express this toward your husband? The next two responses have some similarity and also reflect a common threat that many men struggle with—the fear that they have to change.

"I'd say the greatest encouragement I get from my wife is her unconditional love. My wife allows me to be who I am freely without judgment, criticism, or nagging. It's nice to have a wife who knows how to be a best friend as well. Praise the Lord! She is patient and waits for the right time to talk about things. She never puts me down in front of others."

———

"My wife accepts me just like I am; she doesn't pressure me to change. She greets me when I come home in the evening. She always smiles and seems glad to see me. She seems interested in what I am doing at work. She compliments me on how I dress, she is glad to go places with me, and we enjoy being together. She always trusts me, gives me the benefit of the doubt, and believes the best about me. She is an ideal Christian wife!"

As men go through their struggles in life often it's a woman who helps them navigate the troubled waters. Men may appear self-sufficient and strong, but the reality is we need support.

———

"When my wife notices that I am discouraged or frustrated, she will put her arms around me and pray for me. She thanks me often when I do something around the house. Often, she will leave a Post-it note in a place where I'll find it—and on that note is an encouraging love note. I'm not sure what I'd do in my ministry without my wife. She is a great, great help in many ways in the church. She gives such encouragement just by helping out, contributing her considerable gifts and skill in the church."

———

"She encourages me by being there when I need to express doubts or frustrations. Just to know that she is there and shares common values/interests is a major source of encouragement."

"My wife makes me breakfast every Saturday and Sunday. During the week she puts little notes in my lunch that tell me what she thinks about me."

"With some of the crises that I have been going through, she has been there for me and she knows how much she supports me. Not only in words but also in her actions. With a hug, a soft touch just at the right time, etc. . . ."

"My wife helps me prioritize my activities and schedule. She also helps me to 'lighten up' when I am feeling pressure due to overcommitting my schedule.

"She is also great at counseling me on approaches and strategies to making my activities as focused and directed as possible."

"When I am down my wife encourages me with positive remarks like, 'I know you can do it,' or 'I'll be praying for you.' When she says that she will pray for me that encourages me the most. I know she will, and it gives me the strength and confidence to face another day."

"These are the things my wife does to encourage me:
1. She offers to help me in my work tasks (i.e. visiting, phone calls, word processing).
2. She remembers family dates (birthdays, anniversaries, etc.), obtains presents, cards, reminds me to make phone calls to family.
3. She is a great lover.
4. She is willing to talk over issues and come to an agreement.
5. She is very understanding and forgiving when I disappoint her.
6. She works part-time and brings a salary home that helps the family.
7. She desires me to lead spiritually."

The way in which a woman talks about her husband publicly or in private is important to a man. If a man discovers that his wife has shared intimate details about their life and problems with others, he could be uncomfortable around them. I've been in social situations in which a wife made fun of her husband in front of others; that is extremely painful. Read another encouraging testimonial:

"My wife is always telling me that I have vision and that I'm wise. She also loves to meet with me on my day off to listen to my dreams for the future.

"My wife also encourages me by the way she speaks about me to others. She is complimentary about me to our young daughters. She often tells me when she thinks something I have done is good. She affirms qualities that she sees in me that are positive. It is encouraging to me as she understands what I have to deal with in all the pressures that I feel from so many different angles. It helps when the timing of her requests or conversations don't come when I am dealing with a lot of pressures. I know it's important for me to let her know what I'm dealing with."

The following responses came from men of various ages:

"To encourage me my wife welcomes me when I come home (instead of launching into some huge agenda). She enjoys sexual relations with me (instead of putting it off or showing little interest). She does not depend on me for all her emotional needs. (It encourages me to know she is growing in the Lord and in her friendships with other women.) She is cheerful, or at least able to share humor, even if things are a mess."

"My wife is very supportive, nurturing, and tolerant. She maintains a strong positive attitude. When I talk about things I would like to pursue, she is open-minded. I would gain additional encouragement from her if she would read information on depression and converse with me several times about the status of my coping with depression. This I would greatly appreciate."

"My wife lets me know the good that I did. I think it really helps when she encourages me with specific wording. For instance, I like to hear, 'That speech was great, I really like the way that you put it together. That third point really hit home.' 'Good job!' Instead of 'That was good.'

"She frequently expresses her love for me. Also she

takes pride in what I do and praises me when things go well. She cares about my ideas and will talk with me and be open in her opinions and evaluations. I can ask for nothing more.

"She protects me from people, meaning that she doesn't overcommit me socially. She supports me to others. She does a better job of raising our kids than anybody I've ever seen.

"She thanks me for things I do for her. She compliments me on things I accomplish. She compliments me on my appearance."

"Currently, my wife does several things to encourage me. I value her listening to me the most. She has also affirmed my strengths and praises me when I do something well. Every once in a while she will do that by a note or a card.

"While she tries to listen to me, she doesn't critique me or try to make a point with me when I really need her to listen. That is so helpful."

"My wife and I have only been married a few months. She readily expresses gratitude for things I do around our home, for praying for her, and thinking of her when I am considering a decision that may have an effect on her.

"She frequently tells me the things she likes about me or what I do (approval). If I mention something and am considering something and she likes it, she says so, such as 'That sounds like a good idea.'"

"One of the best things my wife has done for me is to accept her role as helpmate. She desires and strives to make me successful as a husband, father, and business person. She is a quiet and submissive wife but is willing to tell me the things that she feels might be wrong or bad for me to do.

"As a mother of our ten children she has selflessly given up ambitions to excel in the world as a nurse or in other career options. Because she has chosen and dedicated herself to be a stay-at-home mom, she has freed me to provide for my family as God has called and ordered me to do.

"Because she is committed to God, she accepted the challenge to home school all our children. She is a diligent and hardworking woman who has prioritized her life to please God and help me."

"My wife shows affection for me in a tender caring touch or a kiss. She verbally encourages me. She gives respect to our marriage by being faithful to me and comes to church with me even though she may not feel like it. She blesses me when she tells me she wants a baby. This is encouraging me to strive to do better in life."

Many ways of encouraging have been suggested—timing, meeting needs, a cheerful attitude, giving feedback, values, ideas, careful about committing her husband's time, listening, gratitude, affection, and over his appearance.

It was interesting to hear the number of men who were encouraged spiritually by their wives' spiritual responses and involvement.

"She compliments me on my endeavors, she encourages me when I'm down, and she lets me know she loves me no matter what.

"She worships with me, prays and studies with me. She shares a commitment with me that our greatest love is our God.

"She plans and dreams with me."

"My wife is truly the encourager of my life. I will try to explain what I mean in as few words as possible. When I was called to full-time ministry in 1992, I was very apprehensive and fearful. I was doing very well financially, physically, and somewhat spiritually and wanted to reject God's calling on my life. I was doing effective part-time ministry and could not understand why God wanted me full-time in ministry. I consulted my wife, and she encouraged me to do the will of God. Since that day she has been at my side working as my partner in ministry, supporting me financially and with prayers and words of encouragement."

"In my case, it's what my wife is not doing that's been an encouragement. As a professional singer, she has been in demand at other venues which took her away from our home and church on lots of weekends. That brought extra money and fulfillment for her, but it put stress on our marriage.

"About thirteen months ago she began directing and leading a music ministry at our church—actually two of them. Her traveling declined. Coincidentally, our church began to grow significantly.

"In August, our church board voted to hire her as the director of music ministries. She has traveled very little, and the church has seen its greatest growth ever. This has served to encourage me and fulfill both of us. We are working as a team and God is blessing our efforts."

"Knowing that my wife continually and consistently spends personal time alone before the Lord in prayer and Bible study in my behalf gives me mental, physical, and spiritual strength.

"Her complementary attributes and character qualities help me feel a sense of completeness. I know she is the very best mother our children could ever have. Physically, spiritually, socially, even sexually she meets my every need as a helpmate."

"At the present time, my wife encourages me primarily through her faith. She is able to see through our daily struggles, such as finances and overcommitments outside the family, by relying on God's presence in our lives. I typically think to myself her faith is just immature and shallow, but then I realize that would more accurately describe my own faith. She models a faith in her lifestyle that encourages me. Her patience with our fourteen-month-old twins and her gracious understanding of me as I come home stressed and burned out are her primary ways of encouraging me."

To conclude this chapter here are several responses from men who were very appreciative and articulate. Just reading what they said is an encouragement to all of us.

"We have been married forty-one years. My wife has always encouraged me and still does by telling me, 'You can do it' at whatever task I'm embarking on. She also tells me I'm handsome. Also she gives me greeting cards on holidays, birthdays, and anniversaries. For example on the card for my recent sixty-third birthday, she listed on the card sixty-three very complimentary attributes she sees in me. Along with this when I get frustrated or down, she tries to help me see the positive, brighter side.

"She is always willing to join me at golf or fishing, and we both really enjoy the time together. Plus she is always willing to sit and talk over coffee on the deck in the morning or in the winter in front of the fireplace. This helps me to express my thoughts and concerns and helps me move ahead positively.

"I like flying and hunting, and she is always willing to let me go and encourages me to enjoy whichever I'm going to do.

"As for what I would like her to do, I'll be very happy if she just keeps on doing what she is already doing."

"Much of what my wife does to encourage me consists of her conversation. After twenty years of marriage, I have never known her to say anything even slightly degrading about me. This covers our private conversation as well as public. She may disagree with me, or even believe that I am out-and-out wrong, but she always expresses these feelings in appropriate circumstances and in such a way as to let me know that she supports me as her husband. She has the ability to admire the strong qualities of others without ever causing me to feel threatened or inadequate by comparison. Her spoken compliments seem to always spring from some sincere reservoir deep inside, never shallow or trite. Spontaneous, not a matter of rote.

"I am also encouraged by the confidence I have in her faithfulness. She is a beautiful woman and has surely caught the attention of other men. However, she is very cautious of the manner in which she accepts compliments and vigilant regarding the possibility of being placed in any type of compromising circumstance. The fact that she is this way not only releases me from any anxiety in this area, it also increases my sense of worth to know that she holds her relationship with me as very precious."

"It is not so much the grandeur of an infrequent event where I am showered with exclusive gifts and splendid activity but through touches such as praying together, receiving cards in my luggage on a trip, a note of congratulations on the first day of school, keeping mints in the glove box of the car, receiving that special call in the middle of a tough day, an invitation to lunch, a personalized token, a kind word, breakfast or a favorite meal, ensuring that I take my vitamin, get adequate rest and exercise, a friendly reminder that her love is constant and enduring, her commitment to fine grooming, attractive apparel, her soothing fragrance, and earnest prayer prior to our special times together, her diligence in developing that internal beauty that is inevitably manifested externally. Being able to look into the face of one more committed to Jesus than myself and receiving the benefits from that love relationship, her engaging in an upbeat conversation despite the circumstances, her forgiving spirit even when I have blown it, her willingness to refuse to remain angry, but to reconcile and resolve, her commitment to H.O.T. (honest, open and transparent) communication, her disposition that reinforces and leaves no doubt regarding her marital fidelity.

176

her commitment to develop mentally, physically, and spiritually, her willingness to participate on a marital team, the way she loves our child daily, that sparkle of hope that twinkles in her eyes, that radiant smile that inevitably draws a smile in return. It is the accumulation of the small prayerfully crafted and thoughtful deeds that take place daily that ministers to me."

"With my wife, I have received far above what I ever imagined in marriage; hence, I have no expectations other than for Jesus to remain in the center of our marriage ensuring that we increase our love for Him which will naturally result in an increase in our love for each other. (With this, despite the challenges of life, the best is yet to come.)"

It's helpful to hear from these men who are encouraged by the women in their life. What would the men in your life say about the way you are encouraging them? It may be a helpful topic for discussion.

Chapter
9

*Most of us, though, have never really availed
ourselves of a means of power that can change
lives—our own and others.*

Chapter 9

The Power of a Praying Woman

People today are into power. Perhaps it's always been that way. Most of us though have never really availed ourselves of a means of power that can change lives—our own and others. There is tremendous power in prayer.

How are you praying for the men in your life? How do you pray for your husband, boyfriend, father, or son? Would you call yourself a woman of prayer?

God's Word has so much to say to us about prayer. God wants us to talk with Him. He is just waiting to respond.

> "It shall come to pass that before they call I will answer; and while they are still speaking, I will hear" (Isaiah 65:24, NKJV).

> "Then you will call upon Me and go and pray to Me, and I will listen to you" (Jeremiah 29:12, NKJV).

> "Call to Me, and I will answer you, and show you great and mighty things, which you do not know" (Jeremiah 33:3, NKJV).

But we need to understand what prayer is. Stormie Omartian gives us a helpful description:

> Prayer is much more than just giving a list of desires to God, as if He were the great Sugar Daddy/Santa Claus in the sky. Prayer is acknowledging and experiencing the presence of God and inviting His presence into our lives and circumstances. It's seeking the presence of God and releasing the power of God which gives us the means to overcome any problem.
>
> The Bible says, "Whatever you bind on earth will be bound in heaven, and whatever you loose on earth will be loosed in heaven" (Matthew 18:18). God gives us authority on earth. When we take that authority, God releases power to us from heaven. Because it's God's power and not ours, we become the vessel through which His power flows. When we pray, we bring that power to bear upon everything we are praying about, and we allow the power of God to work through our powerlessness. When we pray, we are humbling ourselves before God and saying, "I need Your presence and Your power, Lord. I can't do this without You." When we don't pray, it's like saying we have no need of anything outside of ourselves.
>
> Praying in the name of Jesus is a major key to God's power. Jesus said, "Most assuredly, I say to you, whatever you ask the Father in My name He will give you" (John 16:23). Praying in the name of Jesus gives us authority over the enemy and proves we have faith in God to do what His Word promises. God knows our thoughts and our needs, but He responds to our prayers. That's because He always gives us a choice about everything, including whether we will trust Him by praying in Jesus' name.
>
> Praying not only affects us, it also reaches out and touches those for whom we pray. When we pray for others,

we are asking God to make His presence a part of their lives and work powerfully in their behalf. That doesn't mean there will always be an immediate response. Sometimes it can take days, weeks, months, or even years. But our prayers are never lost or meaningless. If we are praying, something is happening whether we can see it or not. The Bible says, "The effective, fervent prayer of a righteous man avails much" (James 5:16). All that needs to happen in our lives cannot happen without the presence and power of God. Prayer invites and ignites both.[1]

Praying for a man is not a means of gaining control over him. Prayer is a means of transforming people, the one who is praying and the one who is the object of the prayers. Prayer can encourage the one you are praying for, but it can also encourage and change you.

There may be times when it's difficult to pray for that man—it could be your husband. You may *not* want to pray for him. You could be angry or even bitter toward him, and the last thing you want to do is encourage or pray for him. But an amazing thing happens when you bring another person before the Lord. Your attitude begins to change. Bitterness decreases, anger diminishes, hardness toward the other softens. In time you can end up loving the person you are praying for. I've seen relationships restored between daughters and fathers, wives and husbands, and mothers and sons. It may take time, but prayer is the means of restoration, growth, and encouragement.

Stormie Omartian in her most recent book, *The Power of a Praying Wife* shares a struggle that she experienced with her husband's anger.

I began to pray every day for Michael, like I had never prayed before. Each time, though, I had to confess my own hardness of heart. I saw how deeply hurt and unforgiving of him I was. *I don't want to pray for him. I don't want to ask God to bless him. I only want God to strike his heart with lightning and convict him of how cruel he has been,* I thought. I had to say over and over, "God, I confess my unforgiveness toward my husband. Deliver me from all of it."

Little by little, I began to see changes occur in both of us. When Michael became angry, instead of reacting negatively, I prayed for him. I asked God to give me insight into what was causing his rage. He did. I asked Him what I could do to make things better. He showed me. My husband's anger became less frequent and more quickly soothed. Every day, prayer built something positive. We're still not perfected, but we've come a long way. It hasn't been easy, yet I'm convinced that God's way is worth the effort it takes to walk in it.[2]

One of the ways that Joyce has encouraged me over the years is through prayer. When I am traveling and speaking I know that when I call home each evening, I will hear her saying, "I'll be praying for you as you're teaching tomorrow." I'll also find notes stuck in my pockets (and elsewhere!) saying "I'm praying for you" as well as a scripture written out.

Over the years I've made it a practice to pray for my clients each day. I usually let them know that I will be doing this and ask if they have something specific they would like me to pray about during the week. I've had a number of occasions when a person has later shared that the only thing that kept them going was knowing that at least one person was praying for them.

If you're married, what are some ways you could pray for your husband?

Carole Mayhall, writing in *Today's Christian Woman*, suggests the following:

How to Pray "Just for Him":
Make it a point to commit five minutes a day to pray just for your husband. Pray a different scripture for him each

month, as well as other specific requests that God puts on your heart. And keep a prayer list specifically for him. The list might look something like this:

For my husband: (put the date you begin praying)

A. Colossians 1:9–11

- That he would be filled with the knowledge of God's will.
- That he would have spiritual wisdom and understanding.
- That he would live a life worthy of God.
- That he would please God in every way.
- That he would be strengthened with God's power for patience and endurance.
- That he would have a thankful spirit.

B. That he would develop a friendship with a committed Christian who would challenge him.

C. That God would give him a hunger and thirst for himself and his Word.

Write down the answers when they come and date them.

After a friend of mine had been praying specifically for her husband for several months, she called me, excitement lilting in her voice. "Guess what!" she exclaimed. "Bill just told me a new co-worker asked him if he'd be willing to attend a new early morning Bible study, and Bill said YES! And something else. I tried not to show my astonishment when Bill brought home a brochure on a Marriage Enrichment weekend and said he'd signed us up to go."

My friend and I rejoiced together in this new beginning.[3]

A woman shared her story of how God answered prayer for her husband. "While visiting my friend Barbara in Germany last spring, I listened fascinated one evening as her husband Russell,

185

an Air Force officer, explained to a group packed into their dining room about the meaning of the Passover meal we were about to eat. As a Bible study teacher, he had spent hours preparing the lesson, the food, and the table.

"After we'd eaten, I helped Barbara in the kitchen. 'Russ is really turned on to the Lord!' I exclaimed. 'I still remember the Sunday years ago when you asked me to pray for him. He was so wrapped up in his career he had no time for God, and he was so reserved—almost stiff in those days. But now, he is not only a mighty man of God, he's a terrific Bible teacher. What did you do besides pray a lot during the time he wasn't following the Lord?"

As Barbara shared, I jotted down her answers:

1. I had many intercessors join me in praying for him.
2. I was single-minded in my goal—determined that my words and my behavior would make him thirsty for the Lord. I asked the Lord to keep His joy bubbling out of me.
3. Russ liked to show off our home and my cooking by having company over, so I often invited Christians to share meals with us. He enjoyed that—especially meeting Christian men, whom he found fun to be around.
4. The children and I kept going to church.
5. Russ began to go with me to a Bible study—probably out of curiosity, but also because I had such joy. Then he started going to church with the family.

Russ finally decided to make Jesus his personal Lord. He immediately had a hunger to know the Word of God and began spending hours each week studying the Bible. Now he's teaching a Bible study group which meets in their home.

I observed Russell's tender heart toward God during my visit with them, and thanked the Lord for doing such a "good job" in answering a wife's prayers for her husband.[4]

Recently I found a fascinating resource that personalizes passages of Scripture into prayer for a husband and wife. It's called *Praying God's Will for My Marriage* by Lee Roberts. It simply takes passages of Scripture and rewords them. By reading these aloud for a while, anyone could learn to do this for themselves. Here is a sampling:

> I pray that my spouse and I will be swift to hear, slow to speak, slow to wrath: for the wrath of man does not produce the righteousness of God (James 1:19–20).

> I pray that my spouse and I will always love the Lord our God with all our heart, with all our soul, with all our mind, and with all our strength and that we love our neighbor as ourselves (Mark 12:30–31).

> I pray that when my spouse and I face an obstacle we always remember that God has said, "Not by might nor by power, but by my Spirit" (Zechariah 4:6).

> I pray that if my spouse and I lack wisdom, we ask it of You, God, who gives to all liberally and without reproach and that it will be given to us (James 1:5).

> I pray that because freely my spouse and I have received, freely we will give (Matthew 10:8).

> I pray, O God, that You have comforted my spouse and me and will have mercy on our afflictions (Isaiah 49:13).

> I pray that my spouse and I will bless You, the Lord at all times; and that Your praise continually be in our mouths (Psalm 34:1).

> I pray to You, God, that my spouse and I will present our bodies a living sacrifice, holy and acceptable to God, which is our reasonable service. I pray also that we will not be

conformed to this world, but transformed by the renewing
of our minds, that we may prove what is that good and
acceptable and perfect will of God (Romans 12:1–2).[5]

Can you imagine the effect on your relationship when you
literally bathe yourselves with God's Word as a prayer? Try this
for a one-month experiment. Then note the difference.

Since this is a book for women, I thought it best to have
women share their firsthand experiences of praying for men in
their lives. Listen to the variety of ways that God answered
prayer.

> "My youngest son was incorrigible when he was young.
> After trying to handle the problem myself to no avail, I
> handed it over to the Lord and in my mind projected a pos-
> itive image of a successful person—AND IT HAPPENED!!
> Praise the Lord!"

> "As I prayed for my husband it was a gradual process—I was
> a part of a group of women who interceded with me. I can't
> say there was one day everything changed, however, day by
> day, precept on precept, there was a change! Now he is retired,
> and we pray together for our son and daughter. Retirement
> helped bring his focus from his work to our home."

> "I have had several exciting times of praying for a man in
> my life that stand out in my mind. On each occasion it was
> concerning a major life event. The answers God sent gave
> me the peace that a mother and/or daughter needed. I will
> share one with you.

"This prayer time concerned my nineteen-year-old son enrolled at the University of California at Santa Barbara. The time was the height of the Gulf War, and the United States was thinking about passing a law to reinstate the draft of young men. At that point in my son's life, where he was with the Lord and where the Lord was taking him in school, the worst thing in his life would have been to be drafted and taken out of school. Of course, my own heart as a mother cringed at the thought of his being drafted, so I began praying about it and, I might add, pleading with the Lord to protect my son. Several days later, my son called and left a message on my answering machine that he had lost his wallet. It was missing overnight, and he related that he had looked everywhere for it, several times. Now my son lived in Isla Vista, a college town. He said he went back to his car in the morning, and there was his wallet lying on top of the vehicle right where he had probably laid it when he got out of the vehicle. He said, 'Mom, it was just as if God had put His thumb on it' and kept the wallet there till my son came back and saw it. It gave me peace that in the midst of events of the world, God would protect my son. If you know Isla Vista (or any other busy college town), and the number of kids that would be riding bikes by my son's vehicle, you know there would be no way that wallet would still be on top of the vehicle overnight if God had not protected it all day and night."

"After becoming a Christian at the age of twenty-two the desire of my heart was to have a Christian husband. My husband was always loving and kind, but year after year would go by without a commitment to Christ. I prayed and questioned and waited. He always attended Sunday school and morning worship services, but he was not a Christian. Often the Lord reminded me that His timing would come. Eight years later during a revival service, my husband surrendered his heart to the Lord and has joyfully walked with and humbly served Him every day since. The Lord took a truly wonderful marriage and turned it into a glorious one. Praise God!"

———◦

"The greatest miracle we've received is an extraordinary answer to prayer. Four years ago my husband was diagnosed with a malignant brain tumor. After surgery, we were told he would have maybe five years to live. We requested prayer from all our family and friends. It was only prayer that strengthened us each day as God worked in our lives and taught us how to cope and not to fear. We were willing to accept His will whatever it may be. As I watched my once big and strong husband become so weak, I remember once in desperation (or was it selfishness) calling out to God, 'Lord, I want my husband back.' He had always been my protector and my provider, now I was forced to take on so many of his roles. I'm so glad God knows me so well, He understands my temperament and was not offended when I became demanding. God lovingly answered our prayers. To this day my husband is cancer free. I think that surgeon just may become a believer."

———◦

"Sometime after the first grade our son was diagnosed as hyperactive. We knew that he had behavior problems, but now we had a name for his actions . . . only little else in the way of help. The medicine prescribed did not bring about

190

the desired effect, and the doctors could give us little substantive help for how we could deal with his hyper behavior. Since it was 1968 and not many people were familiar with this problem, he was labeled a problem child and I found myself making frequent trips to the school to talk with frustrated teachers who had too many students and limited time and patience for one that was so disruptive.

"As a Christian parent I spent a good time in prayer asking for God's help and wisdom. I knew that my son had a physical problem that was hard for others around him to deal with. Although the doctors assured us that he would improve with the onset of puberty, I could see that his own self-image was probably going to suffer from so much negative interaction with his teachers and other adults. God didn't take away the problem, but He always met my need for help or wisdom for 'next steps.'

"I shared his problem with teachers and listened with understanding to their frustrations with his behavior. Then we made pacts to work together to find positive ways to help him control his behavior. God brought some wonderful teachers into our lives that were more than willing to go the 'extra mile' with us. We shared many successful efforts together. My son is grown up now and married to another answered prayer . . . a steady, solid, and patient Christian woman whom we love and who has given us two special grandsons (both active but not hyperactive!).

"I still pray regularly for my son as well as my other children and grandchildren and he still continues to grow and improve. I can't say I would want to go through those painful times again, but I wouldn't trade the blessing of all the life lessons from that experience. I am so grateful that in spite of the way I feel, God knows exactly when and how to answer my prayers."

"My husband suffers with OCD—Obsessive Compulsive Disorder. When he was diagnosed with this, it was such a crisis for him, he lost his job.

"I began to pray for my husband because there were many times that I felt he was beginning to lose hope, enough to seriously consider ending his life. As difficult as it was for him, I tried to encourage him to know that God was taking us through this crisis for our betterment. The results from prayer have been miraculous to me.

"He is working . . . the doctors said he wouldn't be able to work and would need to be on disability for life.

"We are communicating . . . this is something that we have struggled with in our marriage and have been forced to do to avoid additional stress. We are in counseling together and both of us realize that God is definitely at the controls.

"God does listen. He knows every heartache and pain. He knows exactly what we will encounter. These are some of the things I was able to share with him and still do."

"Every time my husband left to play golf, I grew more and more resentful. It took the better part of a day to play that silly game. A game that seemingly caused him more frustration than enjoyment. I had plans for us together at home. I wanted my husband to be able to relax, but at the same time I wanted him to be a better father to our teenage son. It seemed that my husband wanted only to improve his golf score. Why couldn't he just 'relax' at home? I was jealous that golf seemed to have his full attention.

"I remember one day I brought my resentments to the

Lord in prayer, 'God please help my husband to want to spend more time with our son and me instead of spending so much time away on the golf course.' A picture flashed through my mind of how I wanted God to answer that prayer. I pictured my husband at home with us giving us all the attention that I thought I had earned. I continued my prayer, 'Lord, I believe it is Your will that my husband and I spend time together.' I finished praying, listening for an answer feeling assured that God would side with me, the wounded party. The answer that came was not what I expected. It was almost audible, 'Take golf lessons!'

"The idea followed that instead of me changing my husband, I should instead join him so that I would understand him better. My jaw opened at the very idea of having to bend my schedule any further to accommodate my husband's playtime. But when the thought of taking golf lessons came to me again and again, I began to yield my will to God's and prayed, 'Lord, please provide a way for me to take golf lessons that will work out for all of us.' Several days later, I saw an ad in our newspaper for golf lessons. Two people could take the lessons for the price of one so I enrolled both my son and me. We learned golf's fundamentals, just enough to begin playing. My son and I practiced at a local short course. Our games together turned out to be an unexpected blessing. Time alone on the golf course away from the telephone and television afforded us time to talk and walk through some of the deep issues that teens face. The three of us have played together just a few times, but those days are happy memories. . . . I thank God that His ways are higher than mine."

Perhaps by praying for the man in your life your story could be added here. God does answer prayer. Lives are changed by prayer. What a wonderful way for all of us to be encouraged.

Endnotes

Chapter 1

1. Alan Loy McGinnis, *The Friendship Factor* (Minneapolis, Minn.: Augsburg Publishing House, 1979), 101–2.
2. Robert Sherman, Paul Oresky, and Yvonne Rountree, *Solving Problems in Couples and Family Therapy* (New York: Bruma Mazel, 1991), 27–8.
3. Lee Blaine, *The Power Principle* (New York: Simon & Schuster, 1997), 161–2.
4. Dennis and Barbara Rainey, *Building Your Mate's Self-Esteem* (Nashville, Tenn.: Thomas Nelson Publishers, 1993), 23.
5. John C. Maxwell, *Be a People Person* (Wheaton, Ill.: Victor Books, 1994), 137.
6. Ibid., 134–5.
7. Blaine, *The Power Principle*, 125–6.
8. Ruth Harms Calkins, *Lord, Could You Hurry a Little?* (Wheaton, Ill.: Tyndale House, 1984), 102.
9. Don Dinkmeyer and Lewis Lasney, *The Encouragement Book* (Englewood Cliffs, N.J.: Prentice Hall, 1980), 50–83.
10. H. Norman Wright and Gary J. Oliver, *How to Bring Out the Best in Your Spouse* (Ann Arbor, Mich.: Servant Publications, 1995), 240–7.
11. Dr. Richard Matteson and Janis Long Harris, *What If I Married the Wrong Person* (Minneapolis, Minn.: Bethany House Publishers, 1996), 116–7.

Chapter 2

1. Lewis E. Losaney, *Turning People On—How to Be an Encouraging Person* (England Cliffs, N.J.: Prentice Hall, Inc., 1977), 9–31.
2. H. Norman Wright, *The Power of a Parent's Words* (Ventura, Calif.: Regal Books, 1991), 102–3.

3. Clifford Notarius and Howard Markman, *We Can Work It Out* (New York: G. P. Putnam & Sons, 1939), 28.
4. Ibid., 123–4.
5. H. Norman Wright, *Secrets of a Lasting Marriage* (Ventura, Calif.: Regal Books, 1995), 53–7.
6. Willard R. Harley Jr., *His Needs, Her Needs* (Grand Rapids, Mich.: Fleming H. Revell, 1986), 12.
7. H. Norman Wright, *What Men Want* (Ventura, Calif.: Regal Books, 1996), 118–9.
8. Drs. David and Teresa Ferguson and Drs. Chris and Holly Thurman, *The Pursuit of Intimacy* (Nashville, Tenn.: Thomas Nelson Publishers, 1993), 46–56.

Chapter 3

1. Rainey, *Building Your Mate's Self-Esteem*, 223.
2. Michael Gurian, *The Wonder of Boys* (New York: Putnam Books, 1996), 20–4.
3. Stephen Arterburn and Dr. David Stoop, *The Angry Man* (Dallas, Tex.: Word Publishers, 1991), 58–9.
4. Gary B. Lundberg and Joy Saunders Lundberg, *I Don't Have to Make Everything Better* (Las Vegas, Nev.: Riverpark Publishing Co., 1995), 18–9.
5. Carolyn N. Bushang, *Seven Dumbest Relationship Mistakes Smart People Make* (New York: Villard Publishers, 1997), 86–7.
6. Wright, *Understanding the Men*, 27–31.
7. Ibid.
8. Wright and Oliver, *How to Bring Out the Best in Your Spouse*, 69–71.
9. Wright, *Secrets of a Lasting Marriage*, 122–5.
10. Ibid., 167–8.

Chapter 4

1. Daniel Levinson, *Seasons of a Man's Life* (New York: Ballantine Books, 1978), 332–3.
2. Robert Lewis and William Hendricks, *Rocking the Roles* (Colorado Springs, Colo.: NavPress, 1991), 12–2.
3. Bill Hendricks and Doug Sherman, *Your Work Matters to God* (Colorado Springs, Colo.: NavPress, 1987), 87.
4. John Gray, *Men Are from Mars, Women Are from Venus* (New York: HarperCollins, 1992), 27.
5. Ibid., 20–1; 81.

6. John Gray, *Mars and Venus Together Forever* (New York: Harper Perennial, 1994), 106–48.
7. Wright, *What Men Want*, 112–122.
8. Lucy Sana, *How to Romance the Man You Love* (Rocklin, Calif.: Prima Publishers, 1966), 168.
9. Wright, *What Men Want*, 86–90.
10. Author unknown.

Chapter 5

1. Nancy Groom, *Married without Masks* (Colorado Springs, Colo.: NavPress, 1989), 91.
2. Janet Congo, *Free to Be God's Woman* (Ventura, Calif.: Regal Books, 1988), 47–70.
3. Ibid., 70–1.
4. Bushang, *Seven Dumbest Relationship Mistakes Smart People Make*, 154–68.
5. Barbara DeAngelis, Ph. D., *Secrets about Men Every Woman Should Know* (New York: Delocorte Press, 1990), 23–32.
6. James Walker, *Husbands Who Won't Lead and Wives Who Won't Follow* (Minneapolis, Minn.: Bethany House Publishers, 1989), 100–1.
7. Ibid., 74–5.
8. DeAngelis, *Secrets about Men Every Woman Should Know*, 46–50.

Chapter 6

1. Archibald Hart, *The Sexual Man* (Dallas, Tex.: Word Publishing, 1994), 5.
2. Ibid., 61.
3. Ibid., 78–81.
4. H. Norman Wright, *Holding On to Romance* (Ventura, Calif.: Regal Books, 1987), 130.
5. Ibid., 134–6.
6. Ibid., 180–1.
7. Clifford Penner and Joyce Penner, *Men and Sex* (Nashville, Tenn.: Thomas Nelson Publishers, 1997), 155–6.
8. Wright, *Holding On to Romance*, 200–2.
9. Penner, *Men and Sex*, 158–181.

Chapter 7

1. Howard and Jeanne Hendricks, General editors with LaVonne Neff, *Husbands and Wives* (Wheaton, Ill.: Victor Books, 1988), 277.

Chapter 9

1. Stormie Omartian, *The Power of a Praying Parent* (Eugene, Ore.: Harvest House, 1995), 18–9.
2. Ibid., 17.
3. Carole Mayhall, "The Stale Mate," *Today's Christian Woman,* May/June 1991, 39.
4. Quin Sherver, *How to Pray for Your Family and Friends* (1990, 43–4.
5. Lee Roberts, *Praying God's Will for My Marriage* (Nashville, Tenn.: Thomas Nelson Publishers, 1994), 1, 9, 19, 28, 115, 102, 227, 267.